# LET ME LIVE AGAIN

## The Morning After the Storm

Thomas:
I hope that my life Story
will help you live your life —
after your storm

Rev. Oyd L. Nunez
+
Israel Nunez

# LET ME LIVE AGAIN

## The Morning After the Storm

## Angel L. Nuñez

### with David Alsobrook

# Treasure House

An Imprint of

**Destiny Image® Publishers, Inc.**
**P.O. Box 310**
**Shippensburg, PA 17257-0310**

"For where your treasure is,
there will your heart be also." Matthew 6:21

ISBN 1-56043-310-8

For Worldwide Distribution
Printed in the U.S.A.

This book and all other Destiny Image, Revival Press,
and Treasure House books are available
at Christian bookstores and distributors worldwide.

For a U.S. bookstore nearest you, call **1-800-722-6774**.
For more information on foreign distributors, call **717-532-3040**.
Or reach us on the Internet: **http://www.reapernet.com**

# Acknowledgments

When I invited Evangelist David Alsobrook to come to my church for a three-day revival, I did not expect him to postpone his return for two days just so he could read the rough draft of this book.

After much encouragement from friends, I had begun writing my story more than five years before David came to our church. At the time, it was a rough hodgepodge of recollections with scanty outlines of chapter titles and stories. In fact, I had actually put my efforts "on the shelf" and had grown weary with the effort.

David fell in love with my life story and suggested that I turn it over to him. "Let me see what I can do with it,

Angel. This book deserves a wide readership, and I think I can help it a little."

Soon David was sending proofs to his mother, Dolores (Alsobrook) Scroggins, who, along with Ginny Alsobrook, made valuable contributions to the manuscript. Two of my dear friends and fellow laborers, Frank McGinity and John Rodriguez, each spent long hours proofing and editing the manuscript. I am grateful for the help of each of these persons. Deborah read the chapters and offered insights from her perspective, which further enhanced the book.

The finished manuscript thrills me when I read it. I'm amazed at the way it now flows. To everyone who worked so hard on this book: David, Ginny, Dolores, Frank, John, and Deborah, my heartfelt *thanks*!

# Contents

# Foreword

Over 20 years ago, I attended a ministerial meeting where a noted speaker was addressing a group of pastors. Although I listened to the speaker, I was drawn more to the young man who was interpreting his sermon in Spanish. After the meeting, I went forward and introduced myself to him. He flashed a wide smile and said, "I'm very glad to meet you, Brother Martinez. My name is Angel Nuñez."

I was greatly impressed with this dynamic, young evangelist. As I told my wife, Ana, later, "Angel is a diamond in the rough. He will be greatly used of the Lord with a little polishing." Our friendship blossomed and I could see that Angel had a heart after God and, unlike many young ministers, was totally open to correction and instruction. Whenever I had advice for him, he was open to it. He began looking to me as a spiritual father and befriended me in many ways.

Little did I know, in those early years, that Angel would one day become my son-in-law and father three of our grandchildren in his marriage to our oldest daughter, Deborah. I often had opportunity, in the early phase of his ministry, to watch Angel minister to large crowds of thousands, and my wife, Ana, was frequently called in to assist Angel in his crusades, training altar workers and providing follow-up for converts.

We watched how Angel conducted himself in both his public ministry and his private life, and were close by his side when his first marriage failed. Though deeply hurt, he never reacted in anger or bitterness. My heart was proud of the way he walked through that dark valley, trusting in his Lord without wavering.

During the past eight years, Angel and Deborah have pastored one of our "daughter" churches, the First Spanish Christian Church of Baltimore, Maryland. During this period, Angel has matured in his character and has greatly broadened his understanding of ministry. It is no small wonder to my wife and me that his evangelistic ministry is increasing and his contribution to the local church has helped pastors, who invite him to speak in their churches.

It is our prayer that, as you read Angel's story of pain and sorrow turned into joy and grace, your heart will be drawn closer to the Lord, and the needs in your life will be met.

*Reverend Emilio Martinez*
Pastor, First Spanish Christian Church
Harrisburg, Pennsylvania
Bishop, Bilingual Christian Fellowship, Inc.

**Editor's Note**: Bishop Emilio and Reverend Ana Martinez have ministered in many countries and have raised up several bilingual churches in the United States. Brother Martinez ministered at Teen Challenge Training Center in Pennsylvania as Counseling Division Manager under the oversight of Reverend David Wilkerson for a little more than 16 years. For 30 years the Martinez's have led many drug addicts to deliverance and wholeness.

# Introduction

This book is my contribution to my fellowman. It is my life story. But it is also the story of countless others who suffer today from broken marriages, drug addiction, or child abuse.

Many do not make it to adulthood; they are cut down at a very young age. Others simply exist but have little hope, no dreams, and no vision.

*Let Me Live Again* is a true story about a young boy who lost both his mother and father at a very young age. (His mother died; his father abandoned the family.) He went through hell, and everything inside him died by the time he was a teenager. He had no love, no compassion, and little mercy. Yet God loved him so much that He reached out to him, even though this young man cursed Him.

If you have been hurt or are hurting, this book is for you. If you are angry and have lost all hope, this book is for you. If you are happy and don't have a care in the world, put this book in a safe place: You'll soon be needing it.

I proclaim that Jesus Christ can change any man. No matter what you have been through, He is the answer to your pain. He is the "miracle-maker" and He loves you so! What doctors cannot do, He can do. Who can mend a broken life? Jesus, the Savior of the world!

This book is dedicated to my children: Venus, Georgina, Angela, Israel, and Isaac. I give special thanks to Reverends Emilio and Ana Martinez and Reverend Jesus (Jay) and Selenia Muniz. To Deborah, whom I love with all my being and who has made my life complete, "Thank you, honey"! And most of all to my Lord and Savior, I say, "Thank You, Jesus, for loving me so much! I live to show the world Your everlasting love and the fact that it is through You that I now live again!"

# Chapter 1

# Someday

## *(Age 0-8)*

It was a cloudy morning as we prepared to go to the funeral home. The sun was my dear friend in the tender years of my life, so it was better for me that he was hiding behind the clouds the day we buried Mommy. I could not have tolerated sunshine on the saddest day of my young life.

My sister, Maria, was preparing nervously, and I knew that it was going to be a long day. She had been my strength throughout the past year and a half. Maria was only a year older than I, but she had become a second mother to me while our real mother was ill.

Maria looked much older than her nine years. Her hair was dirty blonde and her light brown eyes were couched upon a very light complexion—a much lighter complexion than is usual for a Puerto Rican. She was the most beautiful sister a brother could have, and I was very proud of her.

Most days Maria radiated her own sunshine, but today her countenance, like mine, reflected only the sadness of Mother's passing. She was not the bubbly ball of energy that usually buzzed around the little apartment we called home. Instead, as she brushed her beautiful hair, she struggled to hold back her tears, as did I. "Hurry up, Angel," she gently coaxed me, "we have to leave soon."

We finished dressing, in our tattered best, for the funeral and in a few minutes were seated in the car on our way to confront our new emptiness. I sat in the back seat and looked at our aunt, Maria Quinones. Aunt Maria dried her tears with a handkerchief. Her brother, tough guy Leocadio Soto, was driving the car with his eyes straight on the road. I could feel Uncle Leo's hurt too. My sister Maria and I sobbed.

The death of our mother, Georgina Soto Nuñez, at the tender age of 34 had taken all of us by surprise because shortly before the end it had appeared that she was getting better. (The doctors had failed to warn us that leukemia victims often experience temporary remission before the disease returns with a vengeance.)

A few nights earlier, I had overheard Uncle Leo crying in his room and couldn't understand how a strong man who never showed any emotion could cry like a child. He sat alone with the door shut, but I could hear his mournful sobs. It was the next day before Maria and I learned the terrible reason for his tears. In fact, they took us to the home of a family friend before they could tell us. This is how difficult it was for Mother's brother and sister to inform us of Mother's impending death.

On the way to the funeral, I lay in the backseat of the car and thought of happier days. I had been blessed to have had the greatest mother any boy could ever want or have. I thought of the countless times we had played in bed, the frequent squeezes and kisses, the continual overtures of love. I remembered how Mother had told me over and over again how much she loved me. Every night she had read me a story, and sometimes when we had the money, she would cook one of my favorite meals.

My first eight years were the happiest years of my early life (until I was born again at the age of 19). Although we were poor Puerto Ricans living in the Bronx, I was alive without a care in the world. Mother, my beautiful mother, was always by my side, and I enjoyed every precious moment of life.

I remember her vividly. Georgina Nuñez had long black hair, dark brown eyes, and a wonderful smile that lit up every room she entered. People loved her for the warmth she radiated to everyone she met.

Mother did not have much money, but she often gave me a nickel for school. Rather than spend it, I frequently saved it. One day I came home and found her crying in the living room. "Mom, why are you crying?" I asked. At first she tried to hide her tears; but when I insisted, she told me that we were not having dinner that evening because we were broke. "Mommy, don't cry," I was happy to tell her, "because I've been saving money in my piggy bank!"

I bolted into my room, broke my piggy bank, and took the money to her. She hugged and kissed me until my cheeks were warm. That's the way my mother was, a caring, affectionate woman with a heart full of love. Mother had always been a faithful churchgoer and was a fine Christian; and even though she was very ill before her death, she spent a great deal of time visiting other sick people and ministering to them as best she could.

I remember something that happened frequently in my very early years. Many times I found Mother in a corner all by herself, in tears. "Mommy, why are you crying?" I would ask. She would pretend that she was fine, but I knew differently. She was crying for my father. Whenever Maria or I asked her when Daddy was coming home, Mother got a faraway look in her eye and always gave the same answer: "Someday he will return."

Our family never heard anything from our father, Angel Nuñez, Sr. It was especially sad to me that I bore the name of a man I never knew. Whenever his name was mentioned, scowls came over our faces. Other family members rarely spoke of him, and when they did, it was to say how bad he was for abandoning his wife and children. Mother was different in

4

her attitude about Dad. She kept waiting for him to come home *someday*. But someday never came...

The brakes screeched, bringing me back to reality. Uncle Leo had stopped at an intersection. I straightened up in my seat in time to notice a young mother leading her two children across the street. I again thought of my family. Why couldn't it have been like that for us too? Why did my mother have to vegetate in a hospital for over a year and then leave us like this?

I turned my head away so no one could see me wiping away my tears. I had to be strong, at least that's what everybody kept telling me. But an eight-year-old boy doesn't feel like being strong at the funeral of the only parent he has ever known.

Looking back after all these years, I remember how I sat in Uncle Leo's car thinking that it was all a bad dream, a nightmare from which I would soon wake up and find Mommy sitting right next to me. But I knew that I was already wide-awake and could not escape the harsh reality of her death. As we pulled up to the funeral home, I remembered the first day these events had all started.

At breakfast that morning, Mom had told us that she had a doctor's appointment and that Aunt Maria would be meeting us after school that afternoon. We got ready to leave for school as always—not knowing how drastically our little family was about to change—and gave Mommy a big kiss on our way out the door. When school was over, our aunt picked us up and took us home. We expected Mother to come home from the doctor's office, but after we had waited and waited, the phone rang. It was Mother. After speaking with her brother and her sister, she asked to speak with us.

I can remember her words as clearly as if she spoke them yesterday, instead of decades ago: "Son, the doctors want me to stay in the hospital for a couple of days. They want me to take some tests."

Amazed that she had to stay longer, I asked, "Mommy, you're not coming home today?"

"No," she replied, "but don't worry. Tell your aunt to give you and your sister ten cents. Go buy some ice cream. I have to go now. I love you, baby. Be a good boy."

I started to cry. She said, "Don't cry. I'll return _someday_ soon."

The days became weeks, and the weeks slowly turned into months. Whenever Maria and I went to the hospital, we were not allowed to see Mother. We had to remain in the waiting area. Our long days were spent waiting for our aunt or uncle to conclude the visit and pick us up. There was a security guard in the hospital, a gentle black man, who kept an eye on us. As time went by, he became our friend. When Mom died, he broke down and cried.

## The Secret Garden

The hospital had a small garden in front that was filled with all kinds of beautiful flowers. I had never seen so many beautiful flowers in one place. This garden became a very special place for me. It was a perfect place: There weren't any dead flowers in it. Bees buzzed from flower to flower just as happy as could be, and birds whistled their beautiful songs—all in this idyllic garden. I retreated there often, thinking that the only thing missing was my beautiful mother. Yes, the most wonderful person in the world, my mother, belonged in this garden. I promised myself that *someday* when Mommy got out of the hospital, I would bring her to this special garden. I would show her all the flowers, tell her the names I had given the birds, and remind her that even as lovely as this garden was, she would always be the most beautiful part of it. We would stand in front of it, have our picture taken, and treasure it forever. But I never got to show her the garden. *Someday* never came.

Mother spent her last year on earth in the hospital. Maria and I saw her only once during that terribly long year, and that was at the very end. When we finally got to see her, we were surprised because we had become accustomed to being allowed only in the relatives' waiting area, passing time in whatever ways we could while our aunt and uncle visited with Mother.

The day we finally got to see Mother began like a typical day at the hospital. We arrived and told the guard that we were there, and Aunt Maria and Uncle Leo went upstairs to see Mother. Our aunt returned shortly and took my sister and me upstairs to a special room. In that room, we were given gloves and masks. After donning them, we were taken to Mommy's room to see her. I couldn't understand what this was all about. All I could think of was my aunt's words that we were going to see Mother.

As we stood outside her room making sure that our masks and gloves were in place, Uncle Leo opened the door and we walked in. There before us was our dear, wasted mother. We wanted to kiss and hug her, but we couldn't because of the masks. She pulled away, and with tears running down her cheeks, asked us to lift the masks so she could see our faces. (It had been over a year since she had seen either of her children.) In that moment of silence, her eyes met ours and told us what words couldn't say...and we three cried. That was the last time we ever saw her alive.

Uncle Leo's car stopped in front of the funeral home, where we saw many people from our church. As we opened the doors of the car, he reminded us that we needed to be strong. With those words, we proceeded to enter the funeral home. My uncle held Maria's hand, while my aunt held mine.

We made our way through the crowd, down a long hallway, and into a big room where Mother's body lay in a casket. A profound silence came over the crowd. My sister and I started to walk calmly over to the body, but Maria suddenly lost control and screamed. She ran over to Mother's casket crying, "Mommy, oh Mommy!" I tried to stay in control, but I couldn't—I just couldn't. I too darted toward the casket, but unlike my sister, I could barely breathe, let alone speak. When air finally came into me, I could only cry in soft sobs. Even after all these years, I cannot describe the pain I felt or find the words to express what happened that day.

8

The cruel reality that my mother, the love of my life, had been stolen from me pierced my heart like a knife. Mommy would never be coming home _someday_. Death, the final separation, had parted us, and she was gone from us forever. I knew that Mommy would have told us that it would not be forever. She would have told her children, could she have spoken from the casket, that we would be reunited in a land where the Light always shines…_someday_. But that thought seemed remote and faraway, like a fairy tale, as I gazed upon her lifeless form.

The funeral directors made us sit down after we had spent a few moments beside her casket. The situation had gotten out of control because the room was filled with people who loved Mother, and they were crying aloud. The directors escorted us to our seats thinking, perhaps, that the scene of the two survivors standing beside the deceased had intensified the emotion in the chapel; but unknown to them was the fact that Mother was deeply loved by all the church, and it showed. It was a moment in which time stood still and pain and hurt filled all our hearts. All I knew was that I wanted my mommy, nothing more. I was eight years old and she was gone, gone forever.

As I sat in my chair crying, I remembered the crusades I had attended in our church and the Bible stories I had heard. I recalled the story of Lazarus and how God had raised him from the dead when Jesus cried out, "Lazarus, come forth!" I said to myself, _If God could raise Lazarus, then He can raise Mommy_. And so I quietly prayed, "God, nothing is impossible for You; so please raise my mother back to life.

I need her." My tears formed streams that were running down my cheeks as the congregation sang hymns. I looked at the casket, waiting for Mommy to get up. But she didn't. I wanted my Mother alive, and nothing else mattered. But God didn't answer my petition. It would be many years before I understood why. That day was a day I will never forget as long as I live. Something inside me died.

I wondered if the sun would ever shine again. I felt alone, nervous, and frightened. *Where are we going to live? What's going to happen to us?* I wondered. I took Maria's hand and held it tightly.

When we finally left the funeral home, my sister and I both knew that we were alone—even though we had aunts, cousins, and my uncle. We were two children alone without a father or a mother...two orphans facing the world. I felt a knot in my throat and started crying again as we got back into the car.

# Chapter 2

# The Windowsill

## (Age 7-8½)

After Mother's passing, the family got into a bitter custody battle over her children. Uncle Leo wanted us to stay with a young couple from the church; Aunt Maria wanted us to live with her. Our older cousins also wanted us to stay with them, and we loved them very much.

Leo and Maria, whose mutual hostility had never abated since childhood, both became selfish in their desires to possess us. For example, Leo dropped us off at school in the morning telling us that he would be waiting to pick us up as school let out that afternoon, and Maria, wise to his plan, would show up in our classroom just before school let out and take us home with her.

11

Their animosities escalated until a big fight developed within the family. For two small children still grieving the loss of their mother, the additional stress of being fought over by two adults became a major problem. It's no wonder I became sick in bed for over a week and little Maria fared no better. We were always changing homes: running and hiding from our uncle half the time when Maria had us, and running from our aunt when Leo had us the rest of the time.

Someone must have reported our situation to the welfare department because one day while we were staying at Aunt Maria's house, social workers showed up without warning and she was forced to allow us to go with them. They took us to a temporary foster home, where we were to stay while the state began the process of looking for a permanent home where my sister and I could grow up together.

Of course our greatest desire was to live together, since our only immediate family was each other. Little Maria was absolutely precious to me, and I to her, but it became increasingly difficult to place us together.

The welfare department had initially decided to separate us. Uncle Leo, knowing how traumatic this would be for us, wisely insisted that we be placed together. (He had a tender side.) So he went to the welfare department and told them how his sister, on her deathbed, had pled with him that her children not be separated. Leo told the officials how he had promised Mother that he would not allow that to happen to us.

The welfare department took Mother's dying request into consideration and began trying to place Maria and me together, but no home was found. Then Leo produced a young couple from Mother's church who offered themselves to the department for consideration as foster parents. By the time Leo found them, my sister and I had already been through three foster homes and were eager to find a permanent home. I will always thank God for Leo's persistence. He became almost frantic in his searching for a suitable home.

You have probably surmised that Mother's brother and sister did not qualify to become our guardians, despite the fact that we had stayed with them during the entire time Mother was hospitalized. Much of what I will relate in this chapter concerning the abusive practices of our aunt and uncle occurred during the time of Mother's illness. It was not only their selfish behavior about their niece and nephew that concerned the welfare officials, but also their violent history. I have no intention of dishonoring any person anywhere in this book, but I need to tell you some things about our aunt and our uncle so that you will be better informed.

Aunt Maria came to live in our home a few years before Mother's passing. (This was before she got her own apartment.) Mother did not invite her sister to live with us; she invited her to come for just a weekend visit. Somehow the weekend turned into weeks, then months, and finally years.

Leo was already living with us prior to Aunt Maria's visit, so our small apartment became quite full. This led to a serious problem because Leo and Maria had never outgrown their sibling rivalry. To say that they did not like each other is an understatement!

They were always fighting with each other—and when I say fighting, I do refer to literal fighting. Some fights became so violent that one or the other ended up in the emergency room of the local hospital! Little Maria and I were disgusted by their example. We could not understand how a brother and sister could treat each other that way.

Their dysfunctional behavior still lingers in my mind. One day just as Leo arrived home from work, he erupted into a serious argument with Aunt Maria. Our aunt not only had a quick temper but was also physically strong. The next thing I saw was our aunt's fist landing squarely on Leo's chest. This angered him so much that he grabbed a mirror and cracked it over her head!

Blood streamed down Maria's screaming face, and Mother fainted at the sight. Then the police showed up and took Aunt Maria to the hospital. All this violence happened in front of my sister and me, and no one made an attempt to shield us from it.

As I said, Aunt Maria had quite a temper. One time we heard a lot of yelling outside our apartment. We lived in the South Bronx, so noise wasn't anything new to us. We often heard people cussing, fighting, and even shooting each other, but this voice sounded familiar, so our attention was alerted. It sounded like Aunt Maria screaming at the top of her lungs!

Mother jumped up, ran to the door, and opened it. What we saw amazed us—we couldn't believe our eyes. Maria was fighting a man who was wielding a knife. She was holding the man's arm that held the knife and punching the daylights out of him with her free fist—even though he was much larger than she was. (She was strong!) As she punched him with all her might, she punctuated her blows with the loudest screams she could muster.

When the neighbors came outside, the bloody-faced robber panicked and ran away. (I'll bet he never robbed another woman!) We ran to help auntie and got her back into the apartment. After we calmed her down, she told us that the man had approached her with his knife, demanding money. When she refused, he tried to grab her large purse; but she did not let it go. Instead she began her own counterattack.

At first we were all amazed by Maria's courage. But when she opened her purse and began pulling out the old newspapers she had stuffed inside, we all looked at her in astonishment. "Maria!" Mother exclaimed. "Do you have nothing in that purse but newspapers? Where is your money? Where are your important papers?"

Aunt Maria reached inside her bra, from which she extracted a little purse. With a triumphant grin, she boasted, "All my money and papers are in here."

Mother, incredulous beyond belief, asked, "Do you mean to tell me that you risked life and limb for an empty $5 purse?"

"Well," Aunt Maria demurred, "I like this old purse and no one is going to take it from me!" (Is it any wonder that the people who lived in our event-filled neighborhood thought our family was particularly odd?)

Another reason our aunt and uncle did not qualify as foster parents was the fact that they were abusive not only to one another but to us as well. When the welfare officials questioned little Maria and me, they must have surmised this from our answers.

After Mother came down with cancer, her brother and sister constantly abused us. Like all young children, we loved toys; but we had precious few of them because Mother could not afford as many as she would have liked to provide. Our aunt never allowed us to play with even the few toys we had.

One Christmas some friends of the family came over and brought some toys for us. My sister received a beautiful doll, and I received a set of toy trucks. We were gleeful! Maria and I played with them intensely, much to the delight of our benefactors. Yet the minute they left, Aunt Maria snatched the toys from our hands and we never saw them again. She explained her actions, saying, "You are bad children who don't deserve any toys."

Children, by nature, love to play; so little Maria and I improvised by making our own toys. Since we had nothing else, we played with bobby pins and small pieces of paper. We learned how to amuse ourselves.

Leo and Maria were not only emotionally and verbally abusive; they were physically abusive too. There were frequent beatings. We were struck with open hands and with closed fists. We were also sometimes beaten with brooms and with belt buckles. On other occasions, Aunt Maria threw hard rice on the floor and made my sister and me kneel on bare knees on the hard kernels for hours at a time.

It was hard for me, but little Maria fared worse than I. No matter what she did, she got in trouble. My sister did most of the housework, with no show of appreciation. She cleaned the apartment, washed clothes by hand, and did everything her aunt demanded. Afterward she was often rewarded with an undeserved beating. Big Maria also terrorized the small girl in ways I will not enumerate here.

Uncle Leo treated my lovely sister a little better, though he whipped Maria many times. He even hit her once with a hammer! To me, my sister was my mother, my confidante, and my best friend, so I hated my uncle and aunt for mistreating her so badly. When I saw the bruises on her little body, I often wished that my aunt and uncle were dead.

Even though the physical abuse was enormous, the verbal abuse and the mind games were even more torturous. For years we lived under a horrible burden of guilt put on us by their insistence that we had put their sister in the hospital and had caused Mother's death. Can you imagine how this made two young children feel? We loved Mother more than any person in the world, and to have authority figures scold us for putting her in the hospital made us feel sick inside. Since no one had explained to us the nature of leukemia, we knew no better.

Aunt Maria, in particular, seemed to delight in screaming, "You killed your mother!" The first time she told us this was a few days after the funeral. Small children have a tendency to believe whatever they are told, so I suffered nightmares from the guilt I was forced to carry.

Maria was a lonely little girl and I was a very lonely little boy. We were allowed neither to have friends come over nor to go to their homes. Since we lived on the fifth floor of our apartment complex, we naturally gravitated to the windows, where we could feel less confined. Often we passed time counting cars as they drove by. I can still remember the emptiness I felt as I sat by the window, looking out at so many people, but knowing that not one of them could enter my world. I was young, but even so I knew that this wasn't the way normal people lived.

One day I was sitting at the window with my elbows on the sill when an uncontrollable urge to sing suddenly welled up within me. The sky was lovely, so I sang to the clouds. The traffic was whizzing below, so I sang to the cars. Passersby were also serenaded, but from my height they could not hear me. Sometimes I stood up and sang to my inattentive audience.

One day a pigeon landed by my window. He cocked his head first one way and then another as I sang to him. Thereafter he would occasionally drop by for another ballad. I believed in my young heart that this pigeon and I became friends, and perhaps he did feel something for me, as I did for him.

The songs I sang were mostly remembered from happier days when I sat beside Mother in her church. I did not understand a lot of the church songs, but it felt so good to sing them. Birds, clouds, cars, and people far away were bellowed words about the love of Jesus. The seeds of the gospel that had been planted in my heart at church were watered at the windowsill. The windowsill was my place of refuge from the constant storms in my life. It was a place where I felt a strange and wonderful peace.

## Pokey and Perky

Maria and I yearned for a pet, but of course we weren't permitted to have one. As I mentioned earlier, Leo, who was often cruel and abusive, also had a tender side to his personality. He showed this side one day when he came home with a bag in his hand. He sat my sister and me down and told us that he had a surprise for us.

Inside the bag were two little chicks. One was for my sister and the other one was for me. Maria scooped up her chick and began kissing it. I too fell in love at once with my chick. I held him gently in my arms, rocking him from side to side. My little chick was a lot like me—small and afraid—but I told him that I would always love him and that he would become my very best friend. I named my chick Pokey, and Maria named hers Perky.

Every morning I jumped out of bed and ran to see my little friend. I kissed him, talked to him, and made him feel so special. He soon grew accustomed to me and was not afraid of me any longer. I missed Mother deeply, and he was like a dear friend who helped me to cope with all the things that were going on. I fed him, played with him, and taught him little things to do. When I came home from school, I would call his name and he would come to me. "Pokey!" I would yell, and soon he'd come running.

One day Maria and I arrived home from school and only Pokey came to greet us. "Where's Perky?" little Maria asked big Maria, who avoided the question and ordered us to sit down for supper.

We were eating chicken soup for dinner. As we ate, Maria kept asking about the whereabouts of Perky. A number of times our aunt told her to be quiet and eat her soup; but finally, wearied by Maria's questions, she replied, "Do you want to know where Perky is? I'll give you one guess. He's in your bowl!"

My sister howled, jumped to her feet, and started gagging. But our aunt just made her sit back down and eat her meal through her sobs and tears. A few weeks later when I came in the door from school, my little friend Pokey did not respond to my calls. We had chicken soup that night as well. After Pokey "disappeared," I spent even more time at my windowsill.

## In the Silence of the Night

This kind of abuse greatly damaged my childhood development and that of my sister. Like all children who suffer repeated abuse, we lost our self-esteem, our minds became warped, and our hearts were shattered into a million pieces with no one in this world to mend them.

I still often ask myself how there can be so many cruel people in this world who inflict hurt on children who are innocent, pure, and full of love—as we were. The perpetual abuse damaged the hoping and dreaming in us that is natural for all children and caused us to simply exist.

We are not alone in this tragic loss. In the silence of the night, children all over the world are crying—crying for a little love, a little peace—and wondering to themselves, "Daddy, Mommy, what have I done to you?" The hearts of these children beg for their parents' love.

Whether I share my testimony in major crusades or in small churches, I always convey to the audience that something in me died the day my mother died. Mother was all my life. Little Maria and I gradually grew to believe that nobody really loved us. Our aunt and uncle did "love" us in their own twisted and cruel way, but it didn't feel like love at all. We were two small children who felt totally alone in this big, wide world.

The welfare department was intent on sending us to a group home in upstate New York, but finally after much debate, the state did accept the young couple Leo had recommended as our foster parents. We were presented to them in a special meeting. They were also Puerto Ricans.

The couple smiled at us, and as the man walked toward us, he introduced himself. "My name is Jay, and this is my wife, Selenia." Jay was taller than most Puerto Ricans, with a sharp and funny sense of humor. We were soon laughing at his jokes. Maria and I both felt at ease with him.

Selenia was the opposite of her tall husband. She was short and had beautiful long black hair surrounding dark-brown eyes. Her countenance emanated firm character, but I could also sense genuine care for us in her heart.

There was something else very special about this couple. At the time I didn't know what to call it, but today I know that their uniqueness was *the love of God* in their hearts.

Years later I learned that Jay and Selenia had been married only a year when they opened their home to two small orphans who were confused, nervous, and somewhat rebellious. I will always thank God for Reverend and Mrs. Jay Muniz. Jay was a natural leader who developed into a successful minister as the years passed. The Muniz's have done mission work with the Native Americans and have pastored for 20 years. Today they pastor a large congregation in Caguas, Puerto Rico.

When my sister and I went to live with them, Jay and Selenia lived in a pretty little house in the Bronx. Actually, it wasn't so little. They rented out the second floor and still had a room for my sister and one for me. Can you imagine how Maria and I felt to have our very own rooms?

I was excited about this new beginning. A year had passed since Mother's death, and I wanted more than anything to have a real home, with a real dad and a real mom. Hope was beginning to spring up in my heart.

Life with Jay and Selenia was very different from what we had known. Jay and Selenia never argued in front of us. There was no screaming, no cursing, and no abuse. There was discipline. We were assigned chores and were not allowed to talk back. When we were punished, we were sent to our rooms.

Unfortunately, Maria and I were not used to discipline. We were rebellious and unruly and had developed a habit of fighting with each other. We messed up the house, disobeyed our foster parents, and challenged their authority. We pushed them as hard as we could, and I guess we tested their patience to the limit. Yet I can honestly say that our foster family truly showed us love, despite our recalcitrant behavior.

One day Maria and I decided not to obey Selenia or to do any of our chores. Taking advantage of the fact that she would not hit us, we provoked her and would not do anything she asked. Selenia, almost in tears, quietly called Uncle Leo. Little did we know that he was on his way. We feared our uncle more than we feared the devil himself because we knew that he was capable of anything when he was angry.

Years before, Maria and I had shut ourselves in our bedroom so Mother could not punish us for misbehaving. We had locked the door, thinking that we were safe from her. We were laughing behind the closed door when Uncle Leo arrived home from work. He got so angry that he took a hammer and broke down the door. When he finally entered the room, my sister and I were holding each other, crying and shaking. We knew that we were going to be severely punished that day, and we were!

But on this day when we were disobeying Selenia, we did not expect to see our uncle. So we continued to put on a show of defiance and disrespect. My sister was yelling at Selenia, reminding her that she was not our mother and therefore could not tell us what to do, when the doorbell rang. Selenia simply got up and opened the door. To our horror, there stood our uncle! He punished Maria first, and I cringed with every sound. Her screams tore me up inside. Then it was my turn. From that day on, we did not dare do anything that would force Jay or Selenia to call our uncle!

Months later, after we had lived with them about a year, Jay and Selenia decided to move back to Puerto Rico. We were not allowed to go with them, so we were to be placed in a foster home in upstate New York, just outside a small town.

We were told that the foster home was a beautiful place where there were horses and all kinds of animals. They also told us that other children who had lost their parents lived in the home as well and promised us that we would be together.

I was excited about the fact that I was going to a place that had all kinds of animals, birds, and even green grass. In the Bronx there are few places where there is green grass, and if you dare to go there, you had better carry a gun.

Maria and I counted the days until our departure. Finally the day came when we were driven to Lakeside Foster Home.

# Chapter 3

# Lakeside Foster Home

## (Age 10-12½)

The trip from the city to the foster home took only a little more than an hour, but to us it was a world away because we had never left New York City before. Our existence had been in "the cement jungle" known as the South Bronx, where numerous buildings were burned down, abandoned cars were junked on every other street, and muggings were a way of life. Added to this were the hordes of roaches and rats that lived with us but never paid any rent!

We turned off the highway and pulled into Spring Valley, a small town near our new home. When we came up to a section of beautiful property where a sign displayed the name "Lakeside," Maria and I got excited.

Lakeside was indeed beautiful. Big trees surrounded a picturesque lake at the front entrance and birds were flying everywhere. There was lots of green grass, but I thought it strange that I didn't see any of the promised horses and cows and wondered where they were. As it turned out, there weren't any. The social worker had lied to me to make moving to the foster home more attractive.

Lakeside was a foster home with approximately 135 children of different ages. Girls had their own cottages and boys had theirs. After our interview with the director of the home, Maria and I were each taken to our respective cottages; and for the first time in our lives, we were separated—although our cottages were only a couple of minutes away from each other. I was not comfortable with the idea of not sleeping with my sister but took it in stride.

The "cottages" were misnamed because they were actually two-storied dormitories, or dorm halls, built on the same pattern as the projects in New York, only much smaller. There were either eight or ten such cottages (I can't be certain) that were kept spotlessly clean by the children who lived in them. We were each assigned chores that had to be performed daily and with excellence. The cottages were divided into two rows. One row of four or five cottages was designated for girls, and the other row, separated from the girls' cottages by a grassy knoll, was designated for boys. At the middle of the partition waved an

American flag that was hoisted high on the pole every morning and lowered every evening.

Each cottage had from 13 to 15 children in it. My sister was placed in a cottage with girls her age, but I was placed in one occupied by older boys because there was no room for me in the cottage for younger boys. This would prove detrimental to my well-being in several ways.

When I arrived at my assigned cottage, I walked up to the second floor, opened the door, and found myself in a long hallway divided into sleeping rooms on both sides. Some rooms were bigger than others. The smaller, more private rooms were assigned to older, more responsible young men who did not require as much supervision.

After leaving the second floor, I followed the director to a large kitchen where everyone was already eating. I was introduced to the "house parent," a tall man in his 50's whom I will refer to as Mr. Smith. He approached me and grabbed me, frightening me by the power of his grip. His wife, on the other hand, was a small woman with a friendly smile.

After dinner the house parents took me to a large sleeping room that had room for four boys and pointed out a bed to me. "This is your bed. Place your things on that bureau," I was instructed. No sooner had I begun placing my things on the bureau then Mr. Smith leaned over and grabbed me again with his powerful grip, reminding me that he was boss and that I would have to answer to him if I did anything out of order.

Later that night as I tossed about in bed and pondered this new place, I couldn't seem to shake the feeling that there was something strange about all this. We had a "father," a "mother," "brothers," and "sisters," but the feeling of family, the love of a family, was not in this place. At least I could not feel any love there. What I wanted most was someone to love me. This was more important to me than trees, lakes, and birds.

There were two unofficial rules in the foster home that every kid came to know. First, the strong kids ruled and the weak kids served. Second, you don't rat on anyone no matter what. If you broke either rule, retribution was certain to follow. To find out where you fit in the pecking order, whether you ruled or served, you had to fight your way up.

This first exposure never changed. After a new kid arrived, someone deliberately picked a fight with him. If he beat up the bully, then he had to fight the next person in line, and so on, until he lost. When the new arrival lost, then everyone stronger than he demonstrated their superiority by beating him up. It was in this manner that the pecking order was decided upon.

It did not take long for me to find out where I was in the strength department. About a week after my arrival, I was walking down to the lake when I noticed a group of kids yelling behind a building. I ran up to the group and saw two guys who were fighting. Not knowing any better, I tried to stop the fight and stood in between them. All of a sudden, a big kid came out of nowhere, told me to mind my own business, and punched me in the mouth. I started crying, and with my mouth full of blood, ran up to my cottage and told my house parent.

What I did not realize was that in one brief moment I had broken both rules. First, I did not fight the kid who hit me; and second, I "ratted" on him. The bully got in trouble, but what happened to me was even worse. Every kid in the foster home started to pick on me! Word got around that I was a little girl who would not fight back. The foster home became a nightmare, a living hell from which I wanted to escape. Every day I got beat up. Even if I fought back, it was to no avail. Somebody was always bigger and stronger than me. Although I was ten years old, I looked like I was six or seven years old. That made me an inviting target.

Meanwhile, my sister was going through much of the same thing with the girls. One day a group of girls cornered Maria in a room and one of them started a fight with her. The difference between Maria and I was that my sister fought back and won the fight. A few days later they got a bigger girl, and Maria beat her up also. Again and again they tried, but Maria gave each one a sound beating until they decided not to test her any longer.

As it turned out, my sister ended up having to fight the guys for me! There was something about my sister that, when she got mad, she didn't care if she had to take on the world— and right about that time, she didn't care! Soon her reputation soared and everybody was afraid of her. I, in turn, was happy because she saved my neck quite a few times. I was very proud that my beautiful sister was so tough!

I was also having problems in my cottage. When the bigger boys, ages 16 through 18, heard the news that the new 10-year-old was a chicken, I soon became the victim of their practical jokes and abuse.

Since I was the youngest, I was required to go to bed at 8:00 p.m. on school nights; the older boys, on the other hand, could stay up until 10:00 p.m. Many nights they would wait until I had fallen asleep and then run into my room with pillowcases filled with books and awaken me with a painful smacking. At other times they made me do their chores, slapped and pushed me, or just whipped on me for the fun of it. They enjoyed having fun at my expense. I learned not to tell anyone because if I did, those guys were sure to find a time to catch me alone and give me the beating of my life.

It was in this environment that I learned to hate. I learned to hate as I never knew that I could hate and wish harm and evil on others. It was in this place that most of the love in me died. I would cry myself to sleep at night, hoping and wishing that someone, anyone, would come and take us away. But no one came.

The home allowed families to visit their children on holidays and at regularly scheduled times, but our family usually could not come because they lived in New York City and had no way to come out to see us. When visiting time came, it was therefore hard on Maria and me. We often waited for family members, hoping against hope that someone would show up; but no one ever came.

Because of all the things I experienced at Lakeside, I often felt like I was in a prison instead of a foster home. I wanted to run away and started looking for ways to escape.

The director of the foster home lived in a big house down the road. We were not allowed to go to his house or even speak to him unless he addressed us first. The only thing I can really remember about him was that he never wanted anyone to walk on the grass. If he caught anyone walking on the grass, the trespasser was severely beaten, even though the director regularly drove on the grass! Everyone was afraid of this man. One thing was clear about Lakeside: *Everyone hit you.* The kids hit you, the house parent hit you, the director hit you, and even the coach, in many ways a caring individual, frequently beat the living daylights out of his athletes.

I hated Mr. Smith, my house parent, more than the others at Lakeside because of his habit of looking the other way while the bigger kids beat me. Whenever we did something he did not like, whether it was against a specific rule or not, he beat us and called us names like "snakes in the grass," "little black monkeys," "spics," "wops," and other names I dare not mention.

One of the few good things about the foster home was that it was indeed beautiful. Lakeside had about 135 acres of land and just about every area was naturally gorgeous— a big improvement over the Bronx! Although there were no horses, Lakeside was the first place I saw deer. There were also all kinds of birds there, many species of which I had never seen in the Bronx. I loved birds and often went bird-watching. My escape from the nasty people in the home was to retreat into the woods and be alone with nature. I'd catch frogs and turtles and keep them in a hidden place I had built in the woods.

I often found an opening among the trees and sat there quietly. It wouldn't be long before I heard birds hopping around me, unaware of my presence, or saw rabbits come near, as did all other kinds of animals, twitching their noses in the air. Beautiful butterflies flew all around the woods and little lizards ran over the forest floor. It was here that I felt at peace—a retreat away from all the hurt and anger, much like the windowsill back in the Bronx, but even better. It was my little "world away from the world," and I enjoyed every minute of it. I always wished that I could stay there all the time, but I knew that I had to return to my cottage and face the meanest of animals found anywhere on the planet.

Besides my frequent retreats into the woods, there was another good thing that happened to me at the home. I stopped having the terrible nightmare that had plagued me since I was eight. This nightmare never changed. In the dream, a giant snake wrapped itself around my body and opened its mouth to bite me. I woke up screaming just about every night. Many times I was afraid to go to sleep because I knew that the snake was coming to get me.

This nightmare had started when my sister and I spent time at our cousin's house. She was a good-looking woman with a bad temper. She was also deeply involved in witchcraft.

Therefore I sometimes thought that the snake in my dream was a spirit sent to torment me.

While my sister and I stayed with this cousin, I saw peculiar things happen in her house that most people would never believe. The most amazing manifestation of the demonic that I ever saw happened when she attended a revival with us at *Christian Mission John 3:16*, the Pentecostal church where my Mother was a member.

## The Revival (Age 7)

*Christian Mission John 3:16* made a big push for this revival. Everyone was encouraged to bring a friend or family member, so we brought our cousin. In the middle of the service, our guest flipped out. She started screaming and kicking, and fell to the floor. Some of the men in the church came running to try to hold her down because they said that she had a demon inside of her. I got as close to her as possible (after all she was our cousin and an invited guest) and will never forget what I saw.

My cousin's eyes were rolled back into her head, and her voice changed to that of a man. Saliva trickled out of the sides of her mouth, and most amazingly of all, she picked up these men with one hand, one by one, and threw them! What made this even more unbelievable was that our cousin weighed about 130 pounds. Yet she was throwing men around like they were dolls. The evangelist, understandably perturbed, came down from the pulpit and walked toward her. The demon inside her let out a scream that penetrated our very souls: "No! Don't touch me you @#%*!."

"In the name of Jesus, I order you to let her go!" cried the evangelist.

"She belongs to me; she is mine," the demon retorted.

"Let her go, I command you, in the name of Jesus!" the evangelist shouted.

It must have been hours before the demons finally left her. (There was more than one.) For a little boy, the experience was unbelievable. I saw the power of satan go to war with the power of God and be defeated right in front of us over and over again. The demons in her cried and pleaded not to be cast out. When that failed, they pretended that they had left, in a vain attempt to deceive the evangelist. But the evangelist was a mighty man of God who refused deception. Eventually the demons all left and everyone rejoiced in the victory of Jesus.

The revival, which had been scheduled to run one week, had to be extended a full month as the mighty power of God was demonstrated night after night. All kinds of miracles occurred. I remember one night in particular. I was standing by the entrance of the church waiting to go to the bathroom, when I noticed a disturbance in the auditorium. The power of God came down so mightily that people were healed sitting in their seats. A blind lady screamed out, "I'm healed! I can see!" A disabled man jumped to his feet yelling, "I can walk, I can walk, I can walk!" Sure enough, he walked.

Soon people everywhere were getting healed. The church was very crowded, so there was not much room for one as small as I to see; but I could see the man walking and other people crying and praising God.

It was at the precise moment that the lame man began to walk that the door of the church swung open and about half a dozen firemen came running in. The head fireman informed the usher, "This building is on fire. You people must leave. Save yourselves!"

The usher calmly replied, "You are mistaken. There is no fire in here."

The fireman insisted, "No, sir, it is you who are mistaken. Flames are pouring out of this building. We were called out because your neighbors saw that the building is on fire. Anyone outside can see the flames."

The usher answered, "Sir, it is you who doesn't understand. There is a fire here, but it is not natural fire. This is Holy Ghost fire direct from Heaven."

The firemen entered the sanctuary and were shocked by what they saw. Some people were dancing in the aisles, others were speaking in tongues, sick people were getting healed, and everyone was praising the Lord.

Although that service occurred many, many years ago, I can still see that group of firemen as clearly as if it was yesterday. When they realized that the fire was of divine origin, one by one they bowed their heads as the head fireman knelt in reverence and humbly proclaimed, *"This is surely the house of God."* I knew then and there that I had witnessed something very special—the power of God on display—and nothing that happened to me in my later years would convince me otherwise.

After my cousin was delivered from the demons, she was told to get rid of all the things she used to practice her black magic. An appointment was made with the pastor to take all her materials and burn them in the church incinerator.

When the day came, she brought everything she could find. The pastor took the paraphernalia and burned everything except one of the dolls she gave him. (He forgot to throw it in while the fire was burning but promised my cousin that he would do so the very next day.)

That night as my sister and I slept in the room next to our cousin, I awoke, startled by a noise. As I opened my eyes, I saw my cousin walking by my bed in her nightgown. Every hair on my body stood straight up because I felt an evil presence. I closed my eyes, hid under the sheets, and didn't move.

The next morning I overheard my cousin telling my aunts that the doll in the pastor's office had been calling her all night. She said that she could see the doll get out of the chair, go to the door, and call her name. She said the cry of the doll was so strong that she got up in the middle of the night and walked down to the church in her nightgown to retrieve it.

One thing I have learned about deliverance over the years is that a pastor, an evangelist, or any Spirit-filled believer can cast out demons. But if the delivered individual lets the evil spirit(s) come back into him, the freedom will be lost.

Many people want to be set free, but they also want to continue to play with fire. It does not work this way. Jesus can set a person free and keep him free, but He will only do that if the individual lets Him.

My cousin was one of the people who choose to play with fire. She did not surrender fully to God but let satan back into her life. Her house was a hotel for demons. My sister and I lived in these conditions for a time. It was there that I started having terrible nightmares. When I arrived at Lakeside and started sleeping in a room with three other boys, somehow my nightmares went away. This was one of the few good things that happened to me at Lakeside.

One afternoon while I was playing in the gym, an African-American boy and I began arguing over a basketball. The argument quickly turned into a fist fight, which was fine with me; but while I was fighting the boy, his brother showed up, started yelling at me, and proceeded to invite himself into the fight. Then in no time at all, about 30 African-Americans assembled themselves against one Latino!

All of a sudden, the kid I was fighting threw a punch and hit me right in the mouth. (I was looking at his brother when he hit me.) Instantly blood spurted out of my mouth, my lips swelled up, and one of my teeth fell onto the floor. Blood flowed over my shirt and down onto my pants.

The gang quickly dispersed while someone helped me to the nurses' station. I dropped into the chair and almost fainted. The nurse attended to my injuries while I cried— not only because of the immense pain I felt, but more because I missed my mother. I kept thinking that I would not be in this cruel place if Mother were alive. Oh, how much I missed her! In her arms I was safe. That was always my favorite place to be. Had she been alive, she would have taken me away from all these horrible people.

These were the thoughts that ran through my mind at the time. But the cold reality was that Mother was not there; I was all alone in a terrible world—a world full of hate, violence, and war. The strong survived and the weak died— and I was weak. I was just a young boy who had lost his mommy and did not know where his daddy was. I didn't know much about rules, hate, or war. All I knew was that I needed love, and my mother was the only person who had ever shown me real love. But she had left me early, and there I was in the middle of this ugly world. I wanted to run, to hide. But where could I go?

I realized there in the nurses' station at the tender age of ten that the only way I was going to survive was to become strong, hard, and cold, like the world I was in. I was going to hurt others. I would become the most violent fighter, willing to go to any extreme. I would not show mercy. But where would I find the courage and strength to become so violent?

It didn't take long to find my answer. I found it in *hate*. I learned to hate everything and everyone. Hate pushed me the extra mile; hate gave me the courage to stand up to everyone, even to the director. I ate it in the morning; I slept with it at night. With hatred as my master, I started to fight back like never before. Even if I lost, I did not care or change. I just hated them all. "One day I will kill them all," I promised myself. "No, better yet, I will torture them and kill them little by little."

I became daring, willing to do anything. I helped start a riot at Lakeside. We broke into cars, attacked the house parents, broke windows, and caused damage to the home. I was very proud of being part of it. I enjoyed the rush that hate and anger gave me and the attention the newspaper coverage afforded us.

Then one day I received some good news. Reverend and Mrs. Muniz had requested that my sister and I go to Puerto Rico and visit with them for the summer, with the possibility of living with them. I was excited about getting on an airplane. I had never been on a plane, and I knew that it would be an adventure. I thought that to fly to another country, away from all this, would be the best thing for me. My sister, on the other hand, was not excited by the news. She had a boyfriend in the home, Alfred, and didn't want to leave him. I, in contrast, was glad to leave—except for the fact that I had not had sufficient time to exact revenge on all my enemies at the home. Nevertheless, anticipation filled my heart.

## Chapter 4

# My First Trip to Puerto Rico

## (Age 12-14)

What most Americans do not realize about Latin peoples living in the United States is that the majority hope, one day, to return to their native country. Even children long to see the place of their familial origins. I was no different.

I counted the weeks and days before Maria and I would be leaving for Puerto Rico. Finally the day came. I arose early and went straight to the director's office, suitcase in hand. I didn't say good-bye to anyone. I was upset that I was leaving the home before I had the chance to hurt someone really badly. I wanted revenge so strongly that I could taste it. But at the same time, this was my opportunity to get away from a prison-like atmosphere, and I was glad to take it. Uncle Leo and Aunt Maria were already at the director's office. After signing some papers, we were on our way to the airport. When we arrived there, I was impressed by the size of the planes. I had seen airplanes in movies, but never up close. They were big.

My heart pounded in my ears. I was impatient to get going. We entered the terminal, and after waiting in line, Maria and I received our boarding passes. We went to the gate and heard the announcement come over the speakers, "Fight 125 to San Juan, Puerto Rico, is ready to board." Soon my sister and I were in the plane taking our seats. (I got the window!) We fastened our seat belts and stared at everything we could see from the plane. After a few minutes we took off, enroute to San Juan, where we would meet our foster parents after a separation of almost three years. The trip lasted three and a half hours. We spent the time playing and looking out the window at the cotton-ball clouds. Finally the plane landed in San Juan.

After being directed to the baggage claim area, we noticed that a great gate stood between us and a multitude of people. No one was allowed inside the baggage claim area except the passengers who were claiming luggage. The people on the other side of the gate looked more like prisoners trying to escape than family members of the arriving passengers. Among them I could see Jay Muniz, with a big cowboy hat and an even bigger smile. He was pointing out which way to go. We got our bags and ran out of the baggage claim area right into the arms of Selenia.

Selenia, as I have noted before, is a beautiful woman. That day she looked exceptionally lovely. She wore a light blue dress and her long black hair was wrapped around her head. She had a gentle smile. There was something about her that always reminded me of Mother. I wasn't sure then what it was, but Selenia was a true woman of God, like Mother had been. I felt like I was coming home, that my new mother (Selenia) was going to be like Mother had been: beautiful and kind. I hugged and kissed her.

"Angel, get your suitcase. We have to go," Jay said. I grabbed the bag and carried it for what seemed like forever, until we reached the car. We loaded the car, got in, and rolled down the windows. Jay then said, "We're on our way to Ponce. Sit back and enjoy the ride. Welcome to Puerto Rico!"

As we left the airport, I could feel the Caribbean sun looking down on us. The sky was a beautiful blue; palm trees were filled with coconuts; the countryside seemed greener than green. This was Puerto Rico, the land of my mother, and I fell in love with it. *Borinquen, tierra de mi madre, te amo.* (Puerto Rico, land of my Mother, I love you!) I stuck my head out the window, looked at the sun, and said, "I'm not leaving this place!"

Jay and Selenia lived in Ponce, a city in south central Puerto Rico. They had rented a house close to the center of the city. Each of us was given our own room, and I immediately fell in love with mine. After we were settled, Selenia called us to the living room, where she reminded us that even though we were staying for only the summer, we would have to behave, do chores, and go to church with them. My sister was not too happy about going to church, but in reality we had no choice. Like Maria, I did not enjoy church; but I was more submissive to the rule than she was.

Living with Jay and Selenia reminded me of the way things had used to be. There was no fighting, no cursing, and no abuse. These people were what I would later call _real Christians_. They spent time with us, took us places, and always tried to do their best for us.

One day Jay came home and told us that he was taking us to his mother's house in Rincon. Rincon was all the way on the west side of the island, so we would have to travel at least two hours to get there. My sister and I were not very excited about going to see Jay's mother, but when Selenia told me that they had horses, cows, and all kinds of animals, I was ready to go.

The very next day we got up early, packed our bags, and in a few minutes were on our way to Rincon. When we reached Mrs. Muniz's house, I was ecstatic with how beautiful the area was. I jumped out of the car and was immediately surrounded by chickens of all kinds: big hens; little chicks with their mothers; and different colored chickens. I had never seen so many chickens in all my life! I started running after them, but they took off so fast that I couldn't catch any of them. Jay called me back and told me to come meet his mother.

Jay's mother was a sickly, elderly lady. The peculiar thing about her, to me, was how she accepted us as family the moment she met us. No questions were asked. She simply received us and loved us as if we were her own. She made food for us, put her arms around us and, yes, even kissed us. I could tell that her love was real.

Jay called for me to come to the back of the house. When I stepped out onto the back porch, I was amazed. The house had been built on a mountain and the backyard was full of all kinds of different trees. Just about every tropical fruit tree you can imagine was there, such as coconut, banana, avocado, and lemon. I felt like I was in the Garden of Eden. I ran around with Jay, picking all types of fruit. We had so many different kinds of fruit we didn't know what to do with them. Jay instructed me to put them in the car so some needy person in Ponce could benefit from the bounty in his mother's yard.

After we ate lunch, I ran after the chickens a little longer until Jay told us to get into the car. After we were all in the car, Jay told us that he wanted to show us something. We started down the mountain, this time driving down the other side. To my amazement, I saw that we were driving right down to the sea! From high up in the mountain, I could see the whole area. The sun was shining on the beautiful blue sea. The water was hitting the white sandy beach. Palm trees surrounded the outskirts of the beach and big white birds were flying all around the area. I had never seen such beauty. It was as if nature stood by itself without the touch of man. The contamination of the

world that I knew seemed not to have touched this magnif-
icent place. It was breathtaking.

We ran out of the car as fast as our feet could carry us.
Soon we were on the beach, running in the sand. Selenia
found a spot and we lay out on the sand to get a tan. As I lay
there, I couldn't help thinking of Lakeside and all the horrible
things that had happened to me since I was a little boy. Again
I looked up to the sky and said, "I'm not leaving this place."

The remainder of our stay in Rincon was short, being a
blur of happy memories. Too soon we were on our way
back to Ponce. Once we returned home, we settled back into
the routine of chores, school, and church.

The church we attended was a small Assemblies of God
church pastored by Reverend Sotomayor, a little man with
big charisma. After attending a few services, my attention
was drawn to a young, pretty girl in the congregation. She
had long black hair and beautiful brown eyes. I fell in love
with her the moment I saw her. Later that evening I asked
Jay her name. He looked at me as if he knew what I was
thinking, but he didn't demean me. "Her name is Naomi,"
he said quietly.

My attitude immediately changed! I enjoyed going to
church. I was the first one in the bath, the first one dressed,
and the only one drenched in cologne. Jay was wise to me
right away. With a knowing smile, he'd frequently remark,
"Oh, it's so good to see how your love for the Lord has
increased, Angel!"

As soon as we arrived at church, I would look for Naomi. Once I spotted her, I kept my eyes trained on her throughout the service. Finally, after a few days, I found the courage to speak to her. I approached her and said hello in the sexiest way I could. She looked me over like I was from another planet and walked away. I was devastated. She didn't even care about me. But I didn't give up. I made up my mind to get her. I showed up at her school. I followed her around at church. I showed up at her house and even made friends with her brother, Noel, who is my age (and who is the subject of the next chapter). She rewarded my persistence by locking herself in her room and not coming out until I had left!

One day Naomi's big sister, Awilda, pulled me aside after church. "Look, Angel, I know that you are a nice kid, and I know that you like my sister. But I must tell you that she doesn't like you."

"Why not?" I protested.

"Because you are a little boy and she is a young teenager."

"Well, I hope you know that I am older than she. So there!" I replied.

"Well, you might be older than she is," Awilda said, "but look at yourself. You are 12 years old but look 8. You don't know how to dress, and you don't even know how to talk to girls."

Her words cut me into a million pieces. I just lowered my head and walked away. I went home and looked at myself in the mirror. *She is right!* I thought. *I don't even have a mustache.*

I tried to get Naomi out of my mind, but one look at her and I went wild. I continued my assault, but she still didn't want to talk to me. One day she turned around and blurted, "I don't like you, I don't want to see you, I don't even want to hear your name. Leave me alone!"

I was brokenhearted over Naomi. I sang all the blues songs on the radio and daydreamed of holding her in my arms and kissing her passionately. I couldn't wake up and smell the coffee, as the saying goes.

One Sunday morning as we left church, I saw Naomi run out and get into Pastor Sotomayor's station wagon. When she saw me approaching, she locked her door and started laughing at me. I looked into the car and saw the pastor behind the wheel. I knew that he would be giving her a ride home and I would not get to say anything to her.

As I tried to speak to her through the closed window, the pastor opened his car door, walked out to the front of the car, and started to speak to one of the members of the church. Naomi was still laughing at me and did not see the pastor leave the car. Immediately I ran to the other side of the car, slid into the driver's seat, placed my arm around Naomi, and asked, "What are you going to do now?" What I did not realize was that in doing all this, I had placed my foot on the accelerator and the engine was racing. The car was in park, but it made such a loud noise that the pastor turned around and saw me in the driver's seat. He must have changed a million colors, but I did not realize that I was pushing on the accelerator. I was too consumed with Naomi.

Finally I turned around and looked out the front window of the car. There I could see the pastor waving his hands in a state of panic. Immediately I took my foot off the pedal and the car came to a smooth idle.

Pastor Sotomayor jumped to the side of the car and pulled me out. He told me a thing or two as we waited for Jay to arrive. While the pastor was scolding me, I couldn't help but glance from the corner of my eye to see where Naomi was. She was sitting in the car laughing at me.

After that incident, I became known as "the kid who almost killed the pastor"! (Looking back, I think about the reputation I got for a love that wasn't reciprocated. Maybe that's why we call young love growing pains.) In any case, I decided to chill out on Naomi for awhile (the coffee pot was warming up!). Summer was passing quickly, and in a few weeks we would have to decide whether we wanted to stay in Puerto Rico or return to the foster home in upstate New York. I had already decided to stay in Puerto Rico, but Maria wanted to go back to her puppy-love boyfriend. I tried to convince her that Puerto Rico was, by far, the better choice, since I wasn't beaten there. I begged, pleaded, and cajoled, but she would not hear it. Alfred was waiting!

I had never been separated from my sister. We had gone through thick and thin together—our Mother's death, our crazy relatives, and the foster home. Maria was not only my big sister but was also like a mother to me. I couldn't understand why she would want to go back to New York if it meant leaving me. Maria was all the real family I had in the world. To think that we would be separated from each other was an impossible thought for me. Nevertheless, for the first time in my life, I had to consider this possibility. I tried to explain to her that Jay and Selenia were the best thing that had ever happened to us, but her mind was set like concrete.

When the day came for us to talk with Jay and Selenia about what we had decided to do, I told them that I wanted to stay. Maria informed them, however, that she wanted to leave. I was heartbroken. The thought of her leaving was inconceivable in my mind. Yet as the final days came to an end, I realized that she was determined to go and I couldn't stop her. I knew, however, that I had to stay.

On the day of Maria's departure we went to the city of Isla Verde to meet some friends who were to take Maria to the airport. I did not see the trees or the animals on the way. All I could think about was my sister's leaving.

When we arrived at Isla Verde, we went straight to the cemetery where Mother was buried. Someone helped us find her grave. I looked at the grave and saw that it did not have a headstone or any flowers on it. Neglected and uncared for, it was dirty and unkempt. To the workers at the cemetery it was just another grave; but for me, the woman buried there had been my life.

"How could they be so cruel?" I asked myself. "How dare they treat my mother's grave this way?" No one could answer my questions. The only sound was that of the wind blowing, and it brought no answer. We stood in silence.

"We have to go, guys," Jay interrupted. I had been so deep in thought while I stood beside Mother's grave that I had not realized that Jay's friends had arrived to take Maria to the airport. For a brief moment, my sister and I faced each other. Then we placed our arms around each other and held tightly. I didn't want to let go; I didn't want her to leave. Still, right there in front of Mother's grave, we said good-bye to each other for the first time in our lives. I was devastated. Choked up, I cried with all my heart. I loved my sister with all my being. She was all that I had left, my everything. As I got into Jay's car and saw Maria leave in the other car, I realized that except for the Muniz's, I would now have to face the world alone. Alone...separated from all blood relatives: my parents, my aunts, my uncle, my sister. Totally alone.

# Chapter 5

# Noel and I

## (Age 12-15)

Living with Jay and Selenia was not a bad deal. I had my own room, helped around the house, and at times even went to work with Jay and helped him on the job. During this time, I also made friends with Noel, Naomi's brother.

Noel was extremely good-looking, with a smile that would get him just about anything he wanted. Even though he was only a few months older than I, he was extremely streetwise. By the time we became friends, Noel had already run away from home once. Jay, being the compassionate man that he is, was trying to help Noel straighten out his life. Therefore, he invited Noel to visit our church. It was there that I first met Noel.

53

I immediately took to Noel because I wanted some insight on his sister, Naomi. (I am a persistent fellow!) He could give me all the information that I wanted on her and tell me how Naomi really felt about me. (I could not bring myself to face the truth that Naomi had been completely honest with me.)

Noel and I hit it off very well, so it didn't take long for us to become good friends. In fact, he became my best friend, teaching me how to ride a bike and encouraging me to fight back whenever anyone tried to pick on me.

Noel liked to fight, no matter how big or strong his opponent was. He just liked to fight, and he was very good at it. One day he looked at me and said, "Angel, you're a little girl. I'm going to make a man out of you." Then without warning, he punched me right in the mouth! I jumped up and began fighting him, which was what he wanted. The good friend that he was, Noel accelerated my training by beating the living daylights out of me! He repeated this "training" numerous times, always ending it with the promise that this type of activity would surely make me tough— and make me tough it did—and that he was doing it because he was concerned for my welfare! Fighting Noel almost every day gave me the confidence I needed to face the bullies in school.

One day as I was standing in line at school, the school's biggest bully came walking down the hall. As he walked by us, he hit each and every one of us on the head with his fist. When he came to me, I said, "If you hit me, I am going to get you back when you are not looking." He laughed at me, hit me on the head, and then turned his back, saying, "Hit me. I'm not looking." Before he could say another word, I was on him. I pushed him so hard that he fell down the stairs and broke his hand. He took me to court, but when I explained to the judge who and what he was, and when the judge saw how big he was compared with me, the case was dismissed.

Shortly thereafter we were again standing in line when the bully showed up and began hitting the kids on the head, as was his custom. This time, however, he was hitting them with the cast that was on his broken hand. When he arrived beside me, he stopped. I looked at him and asked, "Do you want the other hand broken, too?" He didn't say a word, just walked away and left me alone.

As he walked away, I thought back on the decision I had made at Lakeside. I was proud of myself for not having allowed this bully, or any bully, to pick on me ever again.

My reputation spread because of the incident with this bully, which naturally led to more fights. Whenever I got into a fight, I used every dirty trick in the book to win: I hit people with chairs, stuck my finger in their eyes, bit them on the legs, or kicked them between their legs. I was a small, wiry kid and unusually quick. It became clear to everyone in school that if anyone started a fight with me, he'd better be willing to go all the way. "And if you win," I would tell the other guy, "don't turn your back on me. Because the day you least expect it, I am going to stick something into it." I wasn't beyond using knives to help my leverage! After a few more fights, each concluding with decisive wins, no one bothered me anymore in school, and that's the way I liked it.

Somehow word got back to Jay and Selenia that I was fighting in school, getting suspended, and even facing criminal charges. The Muniz's talked strongly to me, punished me, and forbade me to spend time with Noel. The order to stop spending time with Noel was the part I hated most, but I always found a way around the prohibition and constantly managed to get into trouble with Noel by my side.

One day Noel approached my house and sent his secret signal. (It was a song we both knew, which Noel whistled as he rode by the house.) I came out and told him that the coast was clear because Jay and Selenia were not home. Noel was on his bike and asked me if I wanted to go for a ride. I nodded yes, but Noel then did something he had been doing for some time. "The only way I will give you a ride is if you buy a me soda." I, at last, was tired of Noel's taking advantage of me, always charging me to ride his bike because he knew that I didn't own one. What he didn't know, however, was that I had been saving money for some time and had purchased my very own bike. So I told Noel off with a sufficient amount of cursing and ordered him to leave my house. Noel said, "Okay, but you'll come back to me crying and then I am really going to make you pay."

As soon as he took off, I raced inside my house and took out my brand-new bike. I jumped on it and followed him from a distance. He was riding down the street when I passed him as fast as I could pedal. As I breezed by him, I said, "Don't worry, I won't be needing your cheap bike anymore."

The expression on Noel's face said it all. I couldn't help but laugh my heart out. He raced after me and asked me for a ride. I told him that he had to buy me a soda. He did and our crazy friendship was patched up.

I enjoyed life in Puerto Rico a great deal, but church-going was a different matter. When I could not win Naomi's affections, church became a pain. I hated it, but Jay and Selenia demanded that I go with them—and they went every time the doors were open.

The one redeeming aspect of church attendance was see-ing Noel. He, too, was bored with the whole thing, so we found little things to do to spice up our time there. One time we hid the guitar. I remember that evening very well.

We had arrived early when many people were up front praying at the altar. Noel and I were sitting on a bench, whispering to each other. I don't know how we got on the topic of music, but we started talking about the music in the church. I remarked, "You know, that guitar player makes me sick. The old man can't play to save his life and he messes up everything."

Noel answered, "You're right. He makes me sick too. I wish we could get rid of him."

"Why don't we take away his guitar and hide it?" I suggested. Noel agreed that it was a wise plan of action.

The pastor called the church to prayer, and as was our custom, the usher turned down the lights while everyone gathered at the altar to pray. Noel and I quietly walked to the front. No one was looking, so we took the guitar, slipped out of the sanctuary, and hid the guitar in a closet in the hallway. Then we quickly returned to the altar and pretended that we were praying.

When the lights came on, everyone returned to their seats to get ready for the song service. Noel and I watched the old man as he was looking for his guitar. He couldn't find it anywhere. In a matter of minutes, everybody in the church was looking for the guitar. The man was upset, and the poor pastor tried to calm him down. "How could his guitar just disappear?" everyone wondered. We tried to restrain ourselves but couldn't stop laughing. Noel and I were dying when we heard someone yell from the hallway that they found it. In a moment the service started and the old man went back to playing his guitar. Noel and I looked at each other and agreed, "Next time, we'll get him good."

A few weeks later, we got our chance. Everyone was again praying at the altar and Noel and I were sitting on our usual bench, when I turned to him and said, "I got it!"

"You got what?" Noel whispered.

"Let's loosen the guitar strings," I suggested. "When the old coot goes to play, the whole thing will come apart." We both laughed at my witty idea.

Once again, we slipped to the front of the church and pretended to be praying. When we were sure that no one was looking, we took the guitar and slipped out of the sanctuary. Once in the hallway, we loosened all the strings to the degree that the guitar could hardly hold them. Then we slipped back into the sanctuary, replaced the guitar in its original location, and quickly returned to our seats and waited.

It wasn't long before the lights came back up and everyone returned to their seats. The pastor stood behind the microphone, and everyone stood up as they prepared to start the service. We couldn't take our eyes off the old man with his guitar.

As the first song was about to start, the old man ran his fingers through the guitar strings, only to have them all come popping out. We burst out laughing as the old man, with a wild look on his face, tried to put his guitar back together. Because we were laughing so hard, we didn't realize that people were looking at us. It didn't take them long to figure out who was responsible for the guitar's condition.

Noel and I got into big trouble, and everybody in church got mad at us. I thought that Jay and Selenia would stop taking me to church because of this, which was what I wanted, but they punished me at home and assured me that I would still be attending church.

## The Revival in Puerto Rico

One day we were told that a young evangelist, Jorge Raschke, would be visiting our church for a revival. (Today Evangelist Jorge Raschke is one of the most prominent evangelists in all Latin America.) We were encouraged to bring the sick and to invite our friends to attend. I was not interested in inviting anyone, but I was interested in hearing this evangelist.

The last time I had seen an evangelist was the time my cousin had attended church with my mother, Maria, and me (see Chapter 3), and I wanted to see miracles as before. I was not disappointed. When the evangelist came to our church, we saw many kinds of healings with our very own eyes. Noel, too, was deeply impressed by the miracles— especially by the fact that the evangelist emphasized that signs will follow *any* believer, not just an evangelist (see Mk. 16:15-20).

Noel and I took it to heart and decided to give God a try. In fact, as genuinely as I knew how, I gave my heart to the Lord, as did Noel. Then we went up front and asked Brother Raschke to pray for us. *When he put his hands on me, I felt a fire, a burning fire, come over me.* Soon I was at the altar praising and worshiping the Lord. I was also excited, believing that God wanted to use me just as he was using the evangelist. So I said to Noel, "Signs will follow. All we have to do is lay hands on the sick and they will be healed."

Noel replied, "Yes, I believe it too. Signs will follow those who believe!"

After the revival, we decided to put our faith into action. Noel and I took a handful of tracts and started walking around Ponce, telling everyone who would hear us that Christ could heal and save. Nothing stopped us. We had seen miracles and therefore believed that God could do anything. We went into bars, stopped people in the streets, and put tracts in cars, in windows, and in many other places anywhere and everywhere.

One day we went out as usual. I took a bunch of tracts and started down one side of the street, while Noel took a handful and went down the other side of the street. Thus we went down the block, giving out tracts to whomever we found. As we gave out the tracts, we would tell the people, "Jesus saves and heals!"

I came upon a lady who was standing outside her home on a balcony. I handed her a tract, looked in her eyes, and said, "Jesus saves and heals!" She thanked me and started reading the tract. I then continued down the street until I heard her call out to me. I turned around, walked back to her, and asked, "Yes?"

She looked at me earnestly and asked, "Is it true that Jesus saves and heals?"

"Of course Jesus saves and heals," I proclaimed.

"Well, thank you," she said.

I again turned and started to walk down the street, when she called out once more, "Young man, young man!" Again

I walked back to her and she asked, "Is it really true that Jesus saves and heals?"

I looked her straight in the eye and said, "Look, lady, Jesus saves and heals, OKAY?!" Again she said, "Thank you."

I waited a moment, but she seemed not to want to say anything more, so I continued my route. I must have walked ten feet when I heard her voice again, "Young man, young man." By this time I was mad, so I walked back to her and said, "Look, lady, what's your problem?"

"I just want to ask you one more time: Is it true that Jesus saves and heals?" she replied.

"Lady," I said in a nasty tone, "Jesus saves and heals!"

"Okay, if you say so," she answered. Then she gave me a strange look and asked me to come into her house. I called Noel, who was across the street, and signaled for him to come over. Then we both followed the woman into her home. When we entered the house, she asked us to sit down in the living room and told us that she would be right back. Noel looked at me and asked, "What's going on?"

"I don't know," I answered, "but she keeps asking me if Jesus saves and heals. Maybe she wants to give her life to God." Noel and I both got excited at the possibility of winning our first soul to Christ.

After a few minutes, when we heard her returning, we were both ready to tell her the Good News. But what we saw shocked us. For right in front of us sat a little old lady in a wheelchair. (We later learned that she was 92 years old.) The lady I had first talked with looked at us and said, "This is my mother. She can't walk. But if your Jesus can heal her, then let Him heal her. After that I'll let Him save me."

I took one look at the little old lady in the wheelchair and said to myself, "Oh my God! What did we get ourselves into this time?!" Noel was also in shock. He elbowed me and whispered, "This lady can't walk. Look how old she is. She should be in a wheelchair. Let's run out of here."

"We can't leave," I whispered back. "We'll never be able to return to this area if we run." While Noel and I were having our discussion, the little old lady and her daughter were looking at us, waiting for us to do something.

Finally I said to Noel, "Let's pray for her and tell her that she will get healed little by little."

"That's a great idea," Noel answered. "That way, we will look good and can blame the condition on her lack of faith." I stood up and stared at the little old lady. Then I asked her daughter, "Do you have any oil?"

"Well, the only oil I have is cooking oil," she said.

"That's good enough for me!" I answered.

The daughter went to get the oil, while Noel and I started preparing ourselves by praising the Lord. When she came back, I took the oil and poured some on Noel's hand and on mine. Then we placed our hands on the head of the lady in the wheelchair, as we had seen the evangelist do in our

church, and started to pray. We prayed as hard as we knew
how. Even though we did not believe that God would do a
miracle, we still prayed and said all the things we thought
we should say.

After about ten minutes of praying, we decided to stop.
We took our hands off the woman and looked into her eyes,
hoping that maybe, just maybe, something had happened.
But the little old lady looked just as she had before. Nothing
had changed. Well, there was one change: Oil was running
down the side of her head!

All of a sudden Noel raised his voice and said, "I have
not silver or gold, but what I have, I give you. In the name
of Jesus Christ, stand up and walk!" Then Noel moved forward, grabbed the little old lady's hand, and pulled her up.
I joined in and grabbed her other hand as the daughter
exclaimed, "Mother, oh, Mother!" As I kicked the wheelchair to the side, I said to the daughter, " 'Mother,' nothing!
You wanted her to walk? Well, she's going to walk now!"

We started walking around the room with the little old
lady. At first we both held her with our hands. Then Noel
let go of her hand, and finally, I also let go. She started
walking around the room alone, her arms raised up. She
started thanking God for what He had done. She was walking again! The daughter started sobbing and gave her life to
the Lord. Noel and I slapped each other high-fives and
praised the Lord. When we left that home a few hours later,
we said to each other, "Yes sir, Jesus saves and heals!"
From then on we returned to the lady's home every

Saturday to eat ice cream. (Two teenagers learned that serving God brings many blessings!)

This miracle showed me that God was real and that He wanted to use me in a very special way. But I had been backing off from my commitment. I was fighting those inner feelings that go with being an adolescent. The world and all its glory was calling me. I wanted to be accepted by those around me. I wanted to be hip, cool, bad, etc. Most of all, I wanted to have a girlfriend, and Naomi wasn't paying any attention to me. My affection for God waned as the allurements of the flesh pulled me toward the world.

By this time I was 14 years old, and I wanted things my way *now* (not that I had ever bent to the will of others for long). If I didn't get my way, I made life difficult for anyone who blocked me. I am referring, of course, to my godly foster parents, Jay and Selenia. I felt that they were old-fashioned and too strict.

I wrote to my sister and found out that she had married some guy in New York. She invited me to come stay with her, promising, "We can have a great time if you come." I accepted her invitation and convinced Jay and Selenia that I would go visit Maria for only two weeks; but my real intention was not to return. I packed everything I could, said good-bye to everyone, and left Puerto Rico. I was sad about leaving Noel and promised him that I would stay in contact. Little did I know how much closer we would become five years later when I finally returned to that island.

# Chapter 6

# New York City

## (Age 14½-18)

The announcement over the intercom woke me up from my sleep: "The Captain has turned on the No Smoking sign. Please fasten your seat belt, extinguish all smoking materials, and return your tray to its upright position. We will be landing in New York City in ten minutes."

*New York City—my home, my town, my place,* I thought to myself. *I can't wait to get off this plane and see my sister.* Soon the plane landed and pulled up to the gate. Then the airline personnel opened the doors and we all tried to get out as quickly as possible. We walked up a ramp and were soon in a large area where many family members were waiting for their beloved ones. Among them was my sister,

Maria. She yelled out, "Angel! Angel!" and we fought the crowd until we finally made it to each other. Once we met, we kissed each other and hugged like two little kids who had not seen each other in over a year and a half.

Maria looked a lot older than her age, and it wasn't because she had on a lot of makeup. She really looked like a mature woman. I, in contrast, looked like the same skinny, petite boy she had left behind in Puerto Rico. I still looked like I was 10 years old, even though I would soon be 15. Our greeting was interrupted by the voice of a man who said, "Maria!"

Maria let me go, took his hand, and said, "Angel, I want you to meet my husband, Junior." I reached out and shook the man's hand. He was a little taller than I, and he was very well-dressed, tanned, and good-looking. "Pleased to meet you," he said with a smile on his face. Then he turned to Maria and said, "Let's get the luggage. We can't stay here all night. You'll have time to talk at home." With that, we took off like two little children without a care in the world. We were back together again, and this time we would not be separated.

When we arrived at their apartment, we settled my things and Maria went to prepare something for me to eat. Their apartment was small, but comfortable. Junior, who emitted a suave, professional air, had an up-and-coming position at a local bank. (Little did I know that this was a smoke screen.) After I ate, I told them about life in Puerto Rico and that I had promised Jay and Selenia that I would return in two weeks. Maria told me that they did not have the money for my return ticket and that I might have to stay a little longer. This was great news for me because I did not want to return to Puerto Rico anyway. Now I had an excuse. I smiled back and responded, "That's okay with me!" Maria and Junior looked at each other and laughed.

Later that night, I settled in my bed for my first night's sleep back in New York City. As I lay there, I realized that nothing there had changed. At all hours of the night, I could still hear fire engines screaming through the streets of the city, the usual lovers' fights, and shooting all around the neighborhood. The shots sounded like firecrackers popping. Although it was four in the morning, few people in that neighborhood were sleeping—and I certainly wasn't one of them.

I remember how we used to laugh at the commercials on television. They showed pictures of Manhattan, of the Statue of Liberty, and of beautiful bridges and rivers. Then a group of nice-looking people proudly proclaimed, "I love New York," singing the words to a little jingle, and invited people to come to New York to visit.

Well, that was great for them, but if anyone decided to visit our part of New York, he had better come in a tank! In a car, he might never make it out of our part of town. Anyone who parked his car in our neighborhood might return in ten minutes to find his car standing on four milk cartons with no tires, engine, or windows. "Come to New York," the neighborhood gang mimicked, "and leave us your life." Those who knew New York well left the city and tried their hardest not to come back. I, on the other hand, came back to the cement jungle because it was there that I could indulge my fleshly appetites without the restraints imposed by the Muniz's.

Temptation was everywhere, and I was just a kid in this big and mean town. I certainly was not prepared for the trouble that was headed my way, trouble that came by way of my brother-in-law. Junior liked to wear the latest clothing, to play the latest songs on his stereo, and to smoke these little skinny cigarettes that he said would make you feel good (marijuana joints). He was Mr. Cool, doing what he wanted and answering to no one. His refrigerator was always full of beer and he spent most of his free time in nightclubs drinking, smoking, and partying. Maria did not stay behind. She danced all night long, impressing everyone with the way she danced. I didn't know that my sister had such a reputation. They were the ideal couple, Mr. and Mrs. Cool. Maria and Junior really impressed me. I wanted to be just like Junior. It seemed that he had it all: the clothes, the money, the drugs, the car, and the beautiful girl. I admired him.

Due to the teachings I had received in church, part of me wanted to resist this ungodly lifestyle. In fact, before I left Puerto Rico, Selenia had warned me about the temptations that would come my way in New York. She told me that satan would paint a beautiful picture of the world just to ensnare me, and that once entrapped, only God could set me free. I was somewhat scared of the sin I saw, but Junior was slick. He offered me drugs and drinks. He knew that I had been attending church in Puerto Rico, so he made it his business to make fun of Christians. He often said, "Christians can't smoke grass. How sad, because I have something that is going to really turn you on."

Little by little he got to me, until one day I said to him, "Give me that cigarette. I'm going to show you that I can do the same thing you do." So it was that I began a life in drugs at the age of 14. What's worse is that I completely turned my back on God and entered into satan's world of make-believe. I say "make-believe" because that is exactly what it is—an illusion, a lie, a dream that soon becomes a nightmare.

I said to myself, "I want to be like my brother-in-law. I want to drink, smoke, and party all night long. I want to have the girls and the lights, and to be my own man. That's right...my own man!" I started hanging out with Junior. But then, devil that he was, Junior often used me for his own advantage. He gave me stronger drugs so that I would make a fool of myself at parties and afford him and his friends a moment's laughter. I could not control myself because of the powerful drugs. I was Junior's personal clown. After my brother-in-law and his friends got through with me, no one wanted to get near me. I was everybody's fool. Everyone made fun of me and called me all kinds of names. I felt humiliated, and after awhile was too ashamed to come out of the house.

My relationships with girls went down the drain: I didn't know how to speak to them, I didn't know how to dance, and I didn't have any stylish clothing. And of course no girl wanted to date a laughingstock.

71

I went to my sister and told her everything that my brother-in-law was doing to me. Maria became upset and had a terrible fight with her husband. From that moment on, he kept his distance from me. Maria, on the other hand, told me that she was going to show me how to dance and how to treat the ladies. So she made Junior loan me some of his clothing and she took the time to teach me everything I needed to know about women. And teach me she did. She taught me every trick of the trade, and I learned fast.

Soon I started using more drugs. I also made it my business to never again lose my cool. The challenge was to get as high as possible, yet never lose control. (I promised myself to never again let a drug control me.) I would now be in control. I would use more drugs than anyone, including my brother-in-law, yet never lose my cool. This self-deception led me into a stronger drug habit. Of course, I had no money with which to buy drugs. Since Junior and I were "on the outs," I thus had to make money somehow. So I started dealing drugs to support my habit. In the process, I became cold as ice. My heart slowly turned into stone.

The last straw in my relationship with Junior came one afternoon when I was in the park playing handball. I was wearing his shirt and shoes and was having a good time. Then I saw Junior walking toward me. I could tell that he was upset about something. When I asked what was wrong, he raised his voice and ordered, "I want you to take off my shirt and shoes and give them back to me! Right now!" All my friends were looking at me and I felt like dirt. But I sat down on the ground, right then and there, and I took off his shirt and his shoes and gave them back to him. He took them, turned his back on me, and walked away.

There I stood with no shoes or shirt in front of everyone. Once again hatred took total control of my heart. Any love or compassion that I might have had for Junior was lost at that very moment. Due to the sin hardening my heart, I stopped caring for people in general. Something inside me changed for the worse, and I became one of the most violent, cruel, and angry persons you could ever possibly know.

It was not long afterward that my sister divorced Junior. Although he tried everything within his power to get her back, it was of no use. My sister had made up her mind. After awhile, he became a very heavy drinker and only a shell of his former self. Many times I ran into him at parties, only to find him drunk out of his mind, crying and calling my sister's name. Even when he was with other women, he frequently called them by my sister's name, which certainly did not help those relationships! He never got over my sister, and I never cared one whit about helping him in any way. Every time I saw him, I would look at him with disgust and dispose of him, saying: "Leave me alone, fool. I don't want to hear your problems." Junior lost his job, his apartment, his dignity, his reputation, and everything except his breath, after he lost my sister.

As for me, I decided to go back to the foster home. I wrote a letter and asked if they would allow me to return. This was a risk, since they often did not allow re-entry. Soon, however, I received a response telling me that I would have to be interviewed before I would be allowed to return. My desire to return to the foster home was not to get a good education, but to get revenge on those who had hurt me before. I played the game to the "T." In the interview, I promised to do the best I could. I answered the questions the way I knew they wanted to hear them answered.

Not long afterward, I received a letter informing me that I was welcome to return to the home. Two weeks after that I took a cab to Lakeside. The cab pulled up to the director's office and I proceeded to take my things out of the car. As I turned around and looked at the foster home, I had a little grin on my face. _I'm back_, I thought, _and this time all hell is coming with me!_

An hour later I was in my room changing clothes. Then I went out to see some of my old friends. As it turned out, many things had changed at Lakeside during the years I had been in Puerto Rico and New York. Mean Mr. Smith was gone and everybody was walking on the grass because the new director had decided that a more lax policy would improve the home. Smoking, dating, and Friday night parties were allowed. My new house parent, like many others, was on drugs. I loved the new atmosphere!

Some of the kids who had been there before had also left, and new ones had taken their places. Still the two basic rules of behavior had not changed. Once again I would have to fight my way up the ladder. This time I was ready.

It did not take long for someone to pick a fight with me. The kids who remembered me from my previous stay at

Lakeside expected me to cower, as before. Instead, everyone was shocked by my response. I hit the guy with everything I had and didn't have. As far as I was concerned, there were no rules. If you wanted to fight me, you had better be ready for the fight of your life. Rocks, bats, knives—anything was fair. If sticking my finger in your eye helped me, then that was what I did. Word soon got around that I was nuts and was willing to do anything to anyone.

One time a kid started bothering me, so I knocked him out, tied his feet with a rope, and hung him from a tree. I walked away and left him swinging in the air while I went to the play area and began swinging on a swing.

In school at Spring Valley High, no teacher could stand me. I was in the principal's office at least once a week. I cut classes, ran the halls, dealt drugs, and beat up teachers. In just a short time, I became the biggest drug dealer in the area, with my own drug dealers who sold for me. I sold drugs to the house parents, in particular, which gave me power over them. In less than a year, I was making lots of money, had all the girls I wanted, attended all the parties I could, and controlled those people who were in a position to do me any harm. I was now Mr. Cool, cooler than my brother-in-law had ever been, and even as cool as my big-time drug connections. I sold any quantity of drugs, whether 50 pounds of marijuana or 1 pound of cocaine, and any quality as well. I could provide drugs that were pure, "stepped on once," or "stepped on twice," however the customer wanted them. We were all-purpose dealers—of course, at a price! If I did not deal the drugs, then I traded them for other drugs.

We switched drugs back and forth: coke, speed, heroin, acid, hash, grass, opium, and whatever else.

There was only one problem: The drugs I was selling to others were always luring me into addiction. I not only sold drugs; I used them. Since I had access to every illegal drug, I ended up using them all. My only restraint was that I did not want to get hooked on any one drug. Indeed it was a challenge to use the drugs without letting any drug control me. I was successful as far as grass, coke, and acid were concerned, but horse (heroin) was a different story.

I began using heroin by snorting it up my nostrils; in time, however, I turned to mainlining it. Although I had begun using the drug with some regularity, I was oblivious to the fact that I had become hooked—until one day I realized that I didn't have any! In my desperation, I took a hammer and began smashing aspirin so I could heat it and inject it into my veins.

As though a light was suddenly turned on, I realized that I was becoming like some of my friends, who were heroin addicts and had literally destroyed their lives. This could not happen to me. So I decided that I would have to kick the habit once and for all.

I locked myself in my room for three days and three nights. Everything in me screamed for the drug, but I was determined not to be destroyed like so many others had been. I became violently ill—sweating, shaking, and being nauseated—but I refused to lose.

During those days I wrote the following poem:

*NO!*

*Heroin, you call my name and seek my vein.*
*You want to make me one of your many slaves.*

*Your call I will not hear;*
*your power brings me no fear.*

*I cannot live in a world of sadness,*
*but I will not go to a world of madness.*

*I am neither black nor white—*
*I am tan, the color of the sand,*
*and I am proud to say that*
*"I AM NOT YOUR SLAVE!"*

*So leave me be and do not plant your seeds*
*that will bring me to my knees*
*and make me rob and make me kill.*
*'Cause your answer is signed and sealed:*
*NO!*

Even though I was able to overcome heroin addiction, the real me was not changed one bit. I was still very evil, angry, and violent. I still abused people and became further involved with organized crime. One of my former associates was a pimp from New York City, an African-American named Reggie. We were good friends. He often took me with him to Harlem to hang out with friends, do drugs and prostitutes, and of most importance to me, make money.

One day we were with six or seven other mid-level drug dealers in a Harlem apartment, meeting with the "big man"—a major New York City drug dealer. He walked into the apartment and spread a "taste" (sample) of cocaine, commonly known as "coke," on the table. The term "taste" does not refer to a small amount. There was thousands of dollars worth of coke on the table. This was a customary gesture, giving us the signal to dive in and help ourselves to the coke. After we had sampled it, we were to place our order with him, advising him how much we wanted.

Some of us began snorting the coke; others began shooting. Soon different dealers were placing their orders, but I just continued "sampling" the drug, shooting cocaine into my veins. I must have stayed there four or five hours shooting the coke until it was gone. What I did not realize at the time was that I had overdosed.

Reggie took me back to my sister's apartment in the Bronx. (She was not home at the time.) I went in, sat down, and began drifting in and out of consciousness. I was about to die, but seemingly there was nothing I could do about it. Soon I heard loud banging on my door. To this day I don't know how I got to the door, but somehow I managed. It was Reggie. He took one look at me and immediately knew what was happening.

He rushed me to the bathroom, where he stuck my head under the faucet and started shaking and slapping me for an hour or longer, in an effort to make me rouse myself. Reggie's efforts were successful, and I asked him later,

"Why did you return to the apartment?" He explained that I had promised him some grass but had forgotten to give it to him when he dropped me off. So after driving away, he remembered my promise and came back to the apartment to get it. "I called your name, but you did not respond. So I yelled and knocked louder until you opened the door," he explained. I gratefully thanked Reggie, not realizing that it was Someone far greater than he who had spared my life that day.

Not only did I fail to thank God for sparing my life from certain death, but my close brush with death did not change me in any way, except to make me worse! I thought *I* had cheated death and was invincible. (This is the way sin deceives us.) As far as I was concerned, everything was going really well until Tony, one of my dealers, came into the picture.

My drug organization was growing, so I needed more dealers. Tony, who came to me recommended by a friend, did his job well at first. But then he was tardy with a payment and began avoiding me. I sent some of my guys to find him and discovered that Tony had either gone on a drug binge himself, using hundreds of dollars of my drugs, or had sold some of the drugs and kept the money. I was hot.

My guys kept looking for Tony until they found him and brought him to me. "Where's my money?" I demanded. Tony could pay nothing, so I ordered that he be beaten. The guys really tore into him. I walked over to him as he lay on the floor, bleeding, and said, "Tony, in 24 hours you bring me the drugs or the money. I don't care which. If you don't, I will kill you." In my anger, I made a mistake. I should have given Tony three days with that type of ultimatum—time enough for him to scrape some money together—but I didn't.

Tony panicked. He went straight to the cops and ratted on me. They raided my room, found a small stash of drugs (small compared to what I often kept there), and issued a warrant for my arrest. When my informants told me that a warrant had been issued, I called my drug boss. Not wishing to talk on the phone, he advised me to come see him. I went, and he told me everything I was to do. "Go back to upstate New York and turn yourself in. Tell the cops that you are not a pusher but a user, and that those drugs were for you. Tell them that you were hitting on Tony's girl and got into a fight with him over her, and that he made up this crazy story to get back at you. After the judge sets your bail, we'll send bail money to your sister, and she can bail you out. Then a lawyer will get with you and tell you what to say in court. You'll get off easy."

I followed his instructions to the letter. I went back to upstate New York, turned myself in to the authorities, and was taken to jail.

# Chapter 7

# From Jail to Jesus

## (Age 18-19½)

I had never been busted before, but I had heard many horror stories from my associates who had done time. I determined that I would not allow anyone to abuse me in any way and walked tough and cool to my cell.

Much to my surprise, jail turned out to be something of a party. Not that it was fun to be cooped up with only the bare necessities, but something happened that made my jail time easier: I knew just about everyone on my cell block! Over and over I heard familiar voices call out, "Hey, Angel! How's it goin' man?" Soon I was in the groove of things and was making the best of my situation while waiting for my sister to bail me out, according to the plan we had made.

Things did not go as planned, and my rope was tied when Maria, after filing the paperwork, was told that she could not bail me out because she was a few months shy of her twenty-first birthday. This meant that I would have to sit in jail, where it would be harder to prepare for my defense than it would have been on the outside.

The party spirit in me soon died when I realized that I was in *jail* and might end up being there several years if my trial, like my bail, did not go right. I began to worry.

One night as I lay awake on my bunk, I began to look at my life soberly. How was it that a kid who had sang songs about Jesus, had frequently attended church, and had been taught right from wrong could end up in the mess I was in? I thought about it long and hard and began to take stock of my sorry life. *Sorry* is what it was…always looking over my shoulder, never fully trusting anyone, getting hooked on heroin, overdosing on cocaine, and losing any hope of a serious relationship with a girl. Sure, I had plenty of money most of the time, but plenty of headaches as well. Finally I realized the truth about it all: *I was miserable!* Nothing I did and no drug I took brought me lasting satisfaction. I thought about Jay and Selenia—how happy they were. I thought about my mother—how sad she would be if she knew the mess I had made of my life—and for the first time ever I was glad that she wasn't alive to know how her son had turned out.

I was sorry with a capital "S", but not sorry enough not to try and figure out a way to get out of jail. I lay on my bunk worrying about the upcoming trial and what the judge might do to me. If he believed Tony's story over mine, I could end up doing a lot of time. I had been advised by my higher drug connection to lie about the extent of my drug involvement. I would tell the judge that I was new to the scene, that I had bought the stuff the cops found in my room for my personal use, not to sell to others, and that I had been squealed on because I had stolen Tony's girl and he just wanted to get even. But what if the judge didn't believe me? What if one of my other associates got busted before my trial and ratted on me? That would certainly prove me a liar and I would end up doing hard time. *It's no use to worry about that now,* I thought. *I'm sticking to my story and getting out of this rat hole.*

That's the path I chose, and to a large degree, it worked. To my great relief, the judge said that because I was a first-time offender, he would let me off with a three-year probation. But if I got arrested again, I could expect no mercy.

I felt free as a bird! I forgot all about my jailhouse reflections, reasoning that everyone gets depressed in jail, and set about making up for lost time. Although I had been in jail only two weeks, it had seemed like a lot longer with nothing to do but lie on my back and worry about my trial. Now that it was behind me, I got busy making drug deals, doing drugs, and partying.

I later moved back to New York, where I used a number of apartments to keep my drugs and my drug business going. One day I went to one of my apartments to meet one of my dealers. Harold was a black guy and one of my better friends. Was I in for a surprise! When I went into the apartment, Harold was reading a Bible. "Hey, Angel, you used to go to church," Harold called. "What does this mean?" He then bombarded me with questions about salvation.

I got angry, grabbed his Bible, and threw it down. "Forget this stuff. It will mess up your mind!"

Harold reluctantly closed the subject, but a short time later I came upon him again. This time he was in shock. It looked like he was reading a newspaper, so I grabbed it and read: *Christ Is Coming!* "Angel, I don't want to be left behind when Jesus comes," Harold sobbed.

"Listen, buddy. What you and I both need is some R & R. Come with me to Puerto Rico."

On the plane, Harold informed me that he wasn't going to let me do my usual stuff when we landed in San Juan. "We're not going to party. We're going to find out if this God stuff is right," he said. I thought to myself, *Yeah, sure, we'll find out about God*, and chuckled to myself.

But Harold was true to his word. He hounded me when I went to the bars or tried to pick up women. "Don't you know that God doesn't want you doing these things?" he asked. Harold was becoming a real drag! I thought about my old friend, Noel, and found out that he was living out in the country, up on a mountain.

"Harold, let's go see my old friend, Noel. I've told you about him and all the fun he and I used to have when I lived here." (I was secretly thinking that Noel would help me shake Harold out of his religious funk.) So we made our way out to the remote cabin where Noel lived. I would never have dreamed in a thousand years what awaited me there.

*Good old Noel*, I thought, as we knocked on his door. "Hey, Angel!" Noel beamed. "Great to see you again, brother," he exclaimed as he hugged me.

"You don't know how great it is to see you," I replied. Noel and I were naturally speaking in Spanish, which Harold did not understand. So I began translating into English for my black brother.

Then Noel shocked me. "Angel, I've got some wonderful news for you."

"What is it?" I asked excitedly.

"I've been saved! I've given my life to Jesus!"

I was stunned into silence. Harold prodded me, "What did he say?" Sadly I turned to Harold and explained that my long-time friend had given his life to Jesus during my absence from Puerto Rico.

"Can he tell me how to give my life to Jesus? *I want Jesus!*"

"What did Harold say?" Noel asked. I told him and he began, quite literally, to preach to Harold, with me acting as the reluctant interpreter. To my even greater dismay than that of having lost my favorite party friend, Harold responded by falling to his knees and praying the sinner's prayer!

"The whole world is going nuts!" I exclaimed in disbelief. I was angry, really angry, and told Noel and Harold both off. Neither paid any attention to me. They were hugging, crying, and laughing all at the same time. It was sickening— especially since they didn't even understand each other! Finally I stopped translating and left in disgust.

Harold's conversion in Noel's living room made him even worse to be around. Day and night he was reading the Bible, talking about Jesus, telling me I needed to repent, and rebuking me when I wanted to sin. Furthermore, he wanted to attend church all the time with Noel. Noel was attending a Church of God in Ponce, and for reasons unknown to me, I promised to go to church with him the following Sunday "for old time's sake."

Actually, I thought that church would be easier for me to handle than listening to Harold's babbling all the time. After all, church had never gotten to me before. Upon entering the church that Sunday, I chose a seat in the back, thinking that I would go unnoticed. But this time I was in for yet another surprise. All through the song service, there was a feeling in the air that I couldn't shake.

After the song service, the pastor got up and told everybody to hug one another. Harold leaned over and asked me what the pastor had said. "Oh," I replied, "the pastor has asked everyone to hug and pray for one another, that's all." All of a sudden, Harold wrapped his massive arms around me—leaving me completely helpless—and started screaming, right there in the middle of the congregation, "God, save Angel!" Before I knew it, everyone in the church had stopped praying, had turned around, and were looking at us.

I wanted to die and to kill Harold at the same time. As every eye in the church looked at us, I tried to free myself from his embrace, but could not. *This idiot,* I said to myself, *has gone mad and is making a total fool out of me.* But Harold, all the while, just kept on crying and screaming, "God, save Angel!" After about five minutes of this, I was able to get him to sit down; but he refused to let go of me. His tears were falling on my shirt as he continued to cry out to God. The service continued and everyone soon turned around and faced the front. I was so furious that I wanted to jump up and hit Harold. But he just wouldn't let go of me.

Finally an attractive young lady went forward to sing. *This will draw attention away from me,* I thought to myself. But as the angelic-faced young lady began singing, I became even more miserable. Her song was about the Good Shepherd leaving the 99 and going after the 1 sheep that had gone astray.

From where I was sitting, I could see just about the whole congregation. I could see the look in their eyes, and I noticed that they were sincerely happy. They had joy and I did not. All the drugs in the world, all the women, all the money—nothing had given me that kind of joy. As the young lady continued singing, I kept thinking, *Could it be that I am the lost sheep that has gone astray? Is it me?* In the middle of this confusion, I put my hands to my face and noticed tears running down my cheeks. Harold still had his arm around my shoulders, but it no longer seemed to matter. Before I knew it, I was sobbing almost uncontrollably as I felt the love of God drawing me to His heart. I was that lost lamb.

It was like a dam burst inside me. *How can God love me after all the things I've done? How can He care enough for me to reach out to me in love?* All these thoughts came flooding into my heart and mind, yet I knew that it was true. God did love me and was reaching out to me that day. He was offering me forgiveness for all my sins and a home in Heaven forever and ever, where Mother was.

The preacher was well into his sermon before I could get my thoughts collected, but it did no good. It was as though he was preaching right to me. "You must repent of your sins," he bellowed. I knew that he was right.

When the preacher opened the altar for anyone who wanted to receive Jesus, I felt two powerful arms surrounding me. Harold was still hugging me. "God, save Angel!" he begged.

Finally I broke free, went to the front, and knelt at the altar. "God, if You are really real, change me," I prayed.

"Will you give your heart to Me?" an inner voiced asked.

"Yes, I give my heart to You. Change me! Let me live. Let me live again."

Even after all these years, it's hard to put into words what happened that night. Really, I can't describe what the Lord did for me that day. He took me back to my childhood, to Mother, to His love revealed to me as a little boy singing at the windowsill. Then He showed me that all my anger and hostilities were really manifestations of my hurt over Mother's death and my rebellion against His holiness. My heart broke as I wept my way through to salvation at that church altar. My sins were washed away by the blood of Jesus. For the first time in my life, I felt clean inside. It seemed that the weight of the world was lifted off of me. I was free and alive. *Hallelujah!*

When I stood to my feet, I knew that I was a different person. I had become "a new creation in Christ" and "old things had passed away" (see 2 Cor. 5:17). Everything around me looked new. Love filled my heart. I hugged Harold and Noel, feeling closer to them than I ever had in our former sinful lives. We made quite a trio: Three young men who were all excited about Jesus, the Word of God, and telling others about Him.

## How You Can Live Again

Let me tell you about Jesus. He is the Son of God who died for you on the Cross. He wants you. It doesn't matter what you have done or have not done; He cares about you and is waiting for you to come to the end of yourself and begin your life in God. One day Jesus will come again for those who love Him. After that it will be too late. If you don't know Him in a real and vital way, let me urge you to close this book right now and open your heart to God. Ask Him to do for you what He did for me, and your life will also be changed. Jesus loves you and wants to save you.

The Lord has done so much for me. He brought me out of a horrible childhood filled with sorrow and abuse and delivered me from a life filled with sin and crime. You may have a similar story, or you may have had a very happy childhood and a life filled with abundance. Either way, something may still be missing—something that is very important. What you are missing in life—whether you're up or down—is a vital relationship with God. You will never truly live until you draw your life from Him. The Scripture says, "In Him was life; and the life was the light of men" (Jn. 1:4). If you want to live, you must come to the Source of life, Jesus Christ, the Son of God, who promises, "...the one who comes to Me I will certainly not cast out" (Jn. 6:37 NAS).

Let me suggest a prayer. You may not understand all that this prayer means, but God looks at the heart. Just pray it as sincerely as you can:

*God,*
*I have sinned against You and others. I am sorry for*
*my sins and want to change. I believe that You sent*

**90**

*Jesus to bear my sins at the cross. I believe that His sacrifice was pleasing to You and that You raised Him from the dead. I ask that You cleanse me with Your Son's blood. I want to serve You, Lord, and ask You to make me Your child. I receive Jesus Christ as my Lord and Savior. In Jesus' Name. Amen!*

It is important that you get into a good, Bible-believing church that teaches the whole counsel of God, one that believes in the baptism in the Holy Spirit and that expects miracles to happen today. You also need to read the Word of God every day. Let me encourage you to begin with the New Testament, especially with the Gospel of John.

Be sure to write to me and let me know of your commitment to Jesus. I would be most happy to hear from you. You can write to me at:

ANGEL NUÑEZ MINISTRIES
3800 Eastern Avenue
Baltimore, MD 21224

# Chapter 8

# Let Me Live Again

I now need to backtrack and tell you something else that had been going on in my life before I became a Christian. *Today I will meet the love of my life,* I said to myself one bright, sunny day a couple of years earlier when I left the foster home for a trip to New York City to visit my sister, Maria.

She had just moved into her new apartment after breaking up with Junior, and I wanted to spend some time with her. Even more than that, I wanted to meet her new neighbor, a pretty young lady with a little baby girl. Maria had told me all about her on the phone and had piqued my interest.

I arrived at the building and quickly ran up the stairs to my sister's apartment, but she wasn't there. So I decided to knock on her pretty neighbor's door and use the excuse that I was looking for my sister. When I knocked on the door of Maria's neighbor's apartment, a very pretty young lady answered the door. She had beautiful long hair, soft brown eyes, and a very sexy body. I had to catch myself because for a moment, I just stared at her. I couldn't take my eyes off her.

I announced that I was looking for my sister. She informed me that Maria was indeed there and invited me to come in. We all sat around the kitchen table and talked for awhile. I did my best to be Mr. Cool. There was another girl there, but as far as I was concerned, she was grotesquely ugly. (I later learned that she was not really a woman at all, but a man who dressed up like a woman, a transvestite homosexual.)

During our conversation in the kitchen, I tried to get the pretty girl's attention, but the only thing that I really got out of her was her name. "Blanca is my name," she said, "and this is my daughter, Venus." I looked down and saw this beautiful little baby girl. She must have been about eight months old, and I was immediately impressed by how cute and well-behaved she was.

As time went by, I made every effort to get close to Blanca. I got her to go out with me a couple of times, but nothing more developed. Here was Mr. Cool with the ladies, but I went nowhere fast with Blanca. "The right moment will come. Be patient, Angel," Maria advised.

It took a year before Blanca showed any interest in me. This doesn't mean that I was celibate while I was waiting for Blanca. Like many lost guys, I was always in the mood for sex. But Blanca was the girl of my dreams, the one I was waiting for. I was ecstatic when I learned that she had finally broken up with her boyfriend, and I began making all the right moves to get her. The big break for me came when her transvestite friend died of an overdose of drugs. According to the police, the guy was in another apartment in the same building when he took a large number of pills and choked on them. Nobody in the building wanted to identify the body, so I stepped forward and made a positive I.D. for the police. It upset Blanca that so many people knew this man, used him, and partied with him, yet not one of his "friends" had the courage to step forward and tell the police who he was and where he lived. Then again, that's the sorry way we lived in the Bronx. My actions at that sad moment endeared me to Blanca.

In addition to this, Blanca was scared. There were many strange people moving into the building and rumors about a hit or bad drugs were spreading like fire. She was afraid of being alone with the baby in the apartment, so I volunteered to keep her company. Blanca thought that I was such a nice guy. I stayed that night, the next, and the next. My stay lasted 13 years.

We spent some happy times together with only a few minor bumps in the road; but a big problem in our relation-ship developed when the baby got into my drugs and got sick. She was bleeding from the nose and crying. All I did, in my callousness, was tell Blanca to clean her up. She became furious with me and told me off. That fight lasted a month and a half and led to many others. Time and time again, we got into big fights. Finally I moved out of her place. Shortly thereafter I returned to Puerto Rico, where I made a once-and-for-all decision for my Lord and Savior Jesus Christ.

After becoming a Christian, I wrote Blanca a letter. I told her how God had changed my life, that I was no longer using drugs, and that if she gave her heart to Jesus, we could make a life of it. I told her that Jesus was the center of my life now and that I really loved her. She wrote back and told me that she would give it a try. Then a few weeks later, I received another letter telling me that she had given her life to Jesus and that she was willing to come to Puerto Rico and marry me.

We had to wait another four months before she came because I did not have a place for us to live. In fact, I had to build our home, and I did. I worked hard mixing cement, laying bricks, and painting. I saved every cent, worked overtime to buy the furniture and everything else I needed, and poured every spare hour into that house. All I could think about during that time was how our lives would glorify God if we allowed the Lord to be the center of our lives. All I ever wanted, besides glorifying God, was to love someone with all my heart and to be loved in return. I made a promise to God that I would do everything in my power to make up for all the wrongs I had done to Blanca, and that life would be different for us.

Finally our home was finished and Blanca was on her way to Puerto Rico. In a few days, we would be married. I was ready. The trip to the airport was exciting. I couldn't wait to see her. I imagined Blanca running into my arms and kissing me like a crazy woman in love with a man she had not seen in nine months.

The wait at the airport was unbearable. The plane landed at last, and I waited for her to come out of the tunnel. I saw my love and pushed my way through the crowd. "Honey! Honey, it's me!" She turned around, looked at me, and gave me a small peck on the lips. "Get my bags, Angel." That was it. Nothing more. I sensed that something was wrong, but with the crowd pushing, I just turned and followed everyone to the baggage claim area.

As we waited for her bags, I looked at her with tenderness in my heart. She was finally here, to be with me forever. Soon we would be married and all our troubles would end. I caught her eye for just a moment, and as we looked at each other, I noticed something strange in her look. I didn't see Jesus in her. I didn't see a new creature in Christ. Instead I saw the old Blanca, the same person I had left behind…the same bitter, angry person I had lived with for over a year. She pointed to her bag and I retrieved it.

I should have wised up a little, right? No. If I had been dumb about Naomi as a boy, I was an ignoramus now as a man. They say that love is blind. In my case, it was quite stupid too. Little did I realize as I drove from the airport that the next 12 years of my life would prove to be a very mixed bag. On the one hand, Jesus would grow to mean more to me than ever before and would use me to reach thousands of souls. On the other hand, hurts, pain, and discouragement would consume my personal life.

When we finally arrived in Ponce, it was late. I took her to our new home, opened the door, and showed her everything I had built and bought. She was happy, but also tired, so we settled down for the night. I slept in the living room while Blanca and the baby took the bedroom.

A few days later, Blanca and I were married. It was a simple wedding in the pastor's house; by simple, I mean that I didn't even have a ring for her. Every cent I had earned had gone into our home. I hoped that she would understand, and I believed she did. In retrospect, I have wondered about my pastor's counsel. He advised me to marry Blanca as soon as she arrived in Puerto Rico; but I now believe that he would have been wiser to want to meet Blanca and to observe her first both in and out of church. But he was viewing our situation from a practical side. He knew that it would be hard for us to control ourselves since I, at least, was so madly in love. Of course I had not shared with him about Blanca's negative side. My enthusiasm had been so great that I had told him only the good things; so he, quite naturally, advised us to marry quickly so that we wouldn't fall into sin.

After only a few months of marriage, Blanca started complaining about living in Puerto Rico. It failed to meet her expectations, and she said she wanted to go back to New

York. I told her that we could not just up and leave, but that did not stop her from complaining. Every day she would complained about the heat, the bugs, the people, and anything else you can name. Blanca started many arguments with me and tried to make me as miserable as possible so I would hurry us back to New York. While we were in Puerto Rico, Blanca was constantly fighting with this pastor, the church members, and the neighbors. It didn't matter whose feelings she hurt as long as she got her way. After awhile she decided that she did not like church and abruptly stopped attending. I grew weary of making excuses for her. People came up to me and asked for Blanca. At first I did not want everyone in my business, so I made excuses for her. After awhile I continued making excuses, but not with very much conviction or persuasion.

During the last months in Puerto Rico, Blanca became pregnant. This made me happy, as I wrongly believed that a child just might help our marriage. I was also having problems with her daughter. Venus was already five years old. Whatever the girl wanted she got. Blanca would not allow me to correct the child and always reminded me that she was not mine. (Besides, she still had not forgiven me for what happened in New York, even though I had apologized many times for being careless with my drugs.) Venus enjoyed her mother's attitude because she did whatever she wanted, and if I said something that she did not like, all she had to do was cry to her mother and I was in big trouble.

I got so tired of it all that I finally gave in to Blanca and we left Puerto Rico. As we departed, my pastor, with some foresight, said, "Son, one of these days she is going to drive you out of your mind and you will have to leave her."

When we left Puerto Rico, we did not move to New York. I had been in York, Pennsylvania, on a preaching tour sometime before leaving Puerto Rico and had really liked it. When I returned home to Puerto Rico, I made a deal with Blanca. We would leave Puerto Rico, since she insisted; but we would move not to New York, but to Pennsylvania. Blanca agreed, so I went ahead of her and rented an apartment in York; then I returned to Puerto Rico and we all moved to Pennsylvania.

While in York, Pennsylvania, I met the pastor of the local Assemblies of God church there, Reverend Raymond Crespo. He was very friendly and invited us to become members of his church. It was a new beginning for us: a new city, a new home, a new church, and a new baby on the way.

When the baby was born, it was a girl. I remember the doctor coming into the waiting room and telling me that we had a girl. I was taken to a room, given a gown, and taken to see my baby. The doctor showed me this big, fat baby and told me that it was mine. I couldn't believe it, *Wow, what a big baby,* I thought. Just as I was going crazy with my newborn, the nurse came in and told me that the baby I held was not mine. My baby was the little one in the corner of the room. She took the big baby from me and showed me this beautiful, little baby girl with lots of hair. She was very small, just 5 pounds and ¾ of an ounce, but I was so happy: I was in the record books as a father. I suggested that we name her Georgina, after my mother, and Blanca agreed.

On the way out, I gave the doctor a dirty look. This may not have been very Christian of me, but, I mean, the man had just delivered my baby and couldn't even tell the difference between the big baby and my little sweetheart. What a shame!

As time went by, things at home got worse. We were always arguing, having big fights that lasted for weeks, sometimes even months. But the big blow didn't come until I informed her that I had gotten an offer to work at the same center where she was working. (This was before I went into the ministry full-time.) The new job would mean a pay increase for me and the possibility of advancement. Blanca was furious. She said that she did not want to work with me. She threatened me and said that she would quit her job. When I told her that I was going to take the job, and that this time I was not going to give in to her, she stopped cooking dinner for me. She even stopped cleaning the house—all in an attempt to stop me from accepting the offer.

The night before I took the job, Blanca sat me down in the living room and told me the words that shattered my heart forever: "I do not love you anymore." I was in shock. I couldn't believe my ears. I loved her with all my heart, and even though things were hard, I had never expected her to hurt me in such a way. We had problems; but I believed that we could find a solution if we loved each other. Somehow we would make it. But Blanca didn't feel that way. She said that she didn't even love me.

*I have nothing,* I said to myself. Blanca told me that she had stopped loving me while we were still in Puerto Rico, shortly after we were married. How could I have been so blind? In a moment's notice, my world was shattered, my dreams destroyed. Without a word, I just got up and went into the bedroom. After everyone had gone to bed, I went back to the living room and knelt down at the sofa, praying and crying for a very long time. I guess very few people can understand how I felt that day. All I had ever wanted in life was for someone to love me. I thought I had found this love, but that day I realized that I had been wrong. From that day on, pain and hurt were my constant companions. I knew things would never be the same.

What followed were some of the most horrible years of my life. I still took the job, and Blanca made sure that I paid dearly for it. I now had to cook my own food, iron my clothes, sew buttons on my shirt, etc. There was no more, "I love you, Angel" in the mornings or evenings. There were no smiles, no kisses.

I was treated like dirt and felt like it. Venus was forbidden to call me Daddy; my name was now Angel. She was reminded daily that I was not her real father, and that she did not need to ask me for anything.

Blanca repeatedly demanded a divorce, telling me how little of a man she thought I was. She pushed me and pushed me, but I would not give her the divorce she wanted. My self-esteem went down the drain. Everyone knew me as a young evangelist whom God was using in a powerful way. In our crusades, the sick were being healed and the lost were being saved. God was moving through me in a mighty way. Invitations were coming from all over. But I was a hurting man. The thing I wanted most—a family, a wife who loved me for who I was—I did not have.

It's hard to explain, but my pain would ease when I was preaching. I was a different man then. I would cast out demons, heal the sick, and preach the Word with such anointing, it was incredible. But inevitably I would return home to a living nightmare. No one knew my pain; I suffered in silence for so long.

My only peace at home came when I would take little Gina in my arms, climb onto my bed, and play with her for long periods of time. I didn't believe in divorce. Even more than that, I really loved Blanca and I didn't want to let go. A divorce would destroy the family. The girls needed a father, and I never wanted them to suffer the way I had had to suffer without my father.

I was truly a broken man. It was God's gentleness that kept me going. I cried endless nights. I asked God to help me make it. It was His warmth and His words of encouragement when I needed them the most that gave me the strength to go on. Had it not been for the Lord, I would have killed myself or would have lost my mind. But there was still a God in Heaven, and even as the devil sought to destroy my life, I refused to let go of Jesus. I prayed my heart out to God, and He didn't fail me. He was there with me all the way.

It was a living hell, but what could I do? I decided that I would win back Blanca's heart. If there was something there, maybe, just maybe, if she allowed it, God could turn this hell around. I had heard so many stories with happy endings, how God had saved this or that marriage. "Surely," I prayed, "mine will also be the same."

But that was not the reality of my life. We all draw pictures of life and put into them only wealth, health, and success. We forget about failures, sickness, hurts, and closed doors. When it doesn't turn out the way we expected, we are tempted to rebel against God. We blame Him for our bad decisions. But I was determined to win Blanca's heart and to change myself as needed—to correct whatever was wrong in me. I had to save this marriage at all cost.

I tried to understand Blanca, why she was the way that she was. Although communication had never been part of our marriage—we never talked things out—Blanca told me that her mother was in a mental institution, having loved Blanca's father so much that when he left her, she lost her mind. Blanca made it clear that she would never love a man like that. She hated her father for what he had done to her mother and always reminded me that, in her opinion, all men were the same. She often said, "Men just use women; and sooner or later, they leave them."

I tried to get professional help, but Blanca did not want any part of it. I told her that I knew pastors, marriage counselors, and psychologists who could help us, but she insisted that they were all my friends and thus would be partial to me.

Besides, what she really wanted was a divorce, not counseling sessions. So no counseling happened.

Our situation got worse. We couldn't even agree on who might help us. So I continued my personal effort to win her back. I tried to tell her that I loved her, that God was real in my life. I bought her expensive gifts, took her out often, and did everything within my power to win her love. But to her it was all a facade.

I have learned through the years that many young people experience the same thing I suffered. They get involved with someone who has deep emotional hurts and are then unprepared to deal with the resulting problems. They fall in love at such a young age and believe that because they are in love, everything will work out just fine. They expect to live happily ever after. But as I sadly found out, that's not the truth. The truth is that marriage takes much work. Marrying just to get out of the house or the neighborhood, or for any number of other wrong reasons, sets a couple up for more hurts, more pain, and, eventually, more misery— and I mean a lot more misery.

I married a woman who needed a lot of help, and I was never able to find the right way to approach her. Her childhood hurts were so deep that she carried them into our marriage. I often told her that she was punishing me for what her father had done to her mother.

When Blanca's father abandoned his family and her mother lost her mind over it, Blanca's mother had to be placed in a mental institution and Blanca had to be placed in child care at the tender age of two. Although she was a very beautiful young lady when I met her, she was also a very angry young lady; and I, being a man, represented everything she hated. In spite of the deep pain that Blanca had suffered, I knew that Jesus could change her if she would surrender her life to Him. He would heal her broken soul, and a very different woman would replace the one who stood before me. Time and time again I prayed that Blanca would let this happen, but she never did.

On March 1, 1986, as I stood behind the pulpit of _Christian Mission John 3:16_ church in the Bronx of New York City, I turned around and handed the microphone to Reverend Joel Del Toro, the presbyter of the Assemblies of God churches in that area. (This was the church I had attended as a little boy.) Rev. Del Toro took the mike and said, "During these last five days, God has spoken to all of us in a mighty way. He has used His servant to bring fresh water for us to drink. Now I would like all the pastors to come forward, and together with me, pray for Angel and minister to him. Let us pray and ask God to protect him."

As the congregation stood, the ministers made a circle around me, placed their hands on me, and started praying. Although everyone was praying, I could hear the presbyter's voice above the others. He began praying for me, for my ministry, and for my future. Then he began to pray for my family. It was at that precise moment that I felt a sharp pain in my heart. It was so painful that I bent over in pain.

I started to cry, but I couldn't understand why I had so much pain, or for that matter, why I was crying the way I was. It was as if someone had taken a knife, stuck it into my heart, and then slowly cut out one piece at a time.

The pain was unbearable and it took everything I had to stay under control. Finally the prayer was over and I took my seat. As I sat there, I could not shake the feeling that something inside me had broken.

It wasn't until a couple of weeks later that everything exploded. I had just returned home from Houston, Texas. Having the next two weeks off, I settled in my bedroom that evening to watch a basketball game. As I was watching the game, my step-daughter, Venus, came into the room and handed me a note. She said that it was from her teacher, but that she did not want her mother to know. When I read the note, I was surprised to find out that Venus was failing all her classes and that the teacher wanted to see me the next day.

I called Venus back into my room and demanded to know what was going on. Crying, she told me that she had her reasons but was afraid to tell me. After I insisted, she said, "Daddy, it has to do with Mom, and I don't know how you will take it. I just can't tell you."

I said, "Okay, if you can't tell me, then write it down on a sheet of paper. I will pick it up when your mother goes into the shower." She agreed and left the room.

About an hour later, while her mother was bathing, I slipped into Venus' room and retrieved her note. Then I went into my room, sat down on my bed, and opened the note. It read, "Daddy, Mom is having an affair with your friend." I couldn't believe it and immediately went and questioned my daughter further. After being convinced that she was telling me the truth, I returned to my room.

*My wife is having an affair. She is committing adultery with my friend!* As these thoughts pounded through my head, I started shaking. I was becoming blind with rage and couldn't speak. The only thing I kept telling myself was, *Don't lose it, Angel. Whatever you do, don't lose it.*

I started tearing up the room; things went flying. I knew that if I did not get out of there immediately, something terrible was certain to happen. I found my shoes, and was putting them on when Blanca came out of the bathroom. I mumbled something to her and ran out the house. I jumped in my car and took off.

Somehow, I found my way to my sister's house (she, too, had moved to York) and placed a call to my friend, Reverend Emilio Martinez. When he picked up the phone, all I said was, "Please, please, pray for me." My friend sensed that something was wrong, but being a sensitive Christian, he didn't start asking questions; he just prayed for me. Never was the power of prayer so evident to me. He prayed for God to take complete control of the situation and of my being.

As Brother Martinez prayed, I felt as though someone was giving me a tranquilizer, calming me down. When he finished the prayer, I knew that I was in control of myself and that God was right there with me.

My sister was another story. After I hung up the phone, she questioned me at length; and when she found out what had happened, she wanted to go to my house and kill Blanca. I convinced her not to do so, got into my car, and went for a drive.

A thousand things ran through my mind. *How can she do this to me?* I asked myself. I felt betrayed. I felt like I was nothing. The pain in my heart came back to me again, the same pain I had felt at the altar in New York City as the presbyter prayed for me. I pulled my car to the side of the road and cried as I had not cried since the death of my mother. I finally realized that Blanca really didn't love me in any sense of the word.

That night I didn't go home for a long time. When I did go home, I was hoping that whatever had happened between Blanca and my friend was not as bad as I had been led to believe. I was also hoping that Blanca would admit her sin and ask for forgiveness, then I would forgive her and all would be well with us.

It's a shame, isn't it? Whenever you love someone who doesn't love you in return, you tend to be so blind to what is happening, always looking for excuses to justify your beloved's wrong behavior, always reasoning everything in their favor, always hoping that the next day will be different. What really happens is that you become a participant in the abuse cycle and are guilty of allowing it to continue. This is what happened to me. I understand now, in hindsight, that I had become codependent on Blanca, and both of us were the worse for it.

Let me be clear about this. God could have changed Blanca had she wanted to be changed. He can change the most degraded person. Yet He will not change anyone who does not want to change. That is, the Holy Spirit will not enter where He is not invited. God will not force anyone to serve Him; He will not violate any person's choices. In view of Blanca's resistance to God, I set us up for repeated abuse and eventual failure because I insisted that she would change if only I prayed long enough.

It's time we all woke up and realized that there is enough pain and suffering to go around without our adding to it and then justifying it by saying, "I'm suffering for the Lord." Having said this, I will also state that my God is a God of miracles, that nothing is impossible with Him. God can make a way, but not every situation has a happy ending. Some of us must drink the cup of suffering like our Master did, and accept the will of God in spite of our negative experiences.

In the Book of Acts, we see two entirely different outcomes in similar negative experiences. The Word tells us the stories of Peter and of James. We always love to hear how God liberated Peter from the hands of Herod and what a mighty display of power He wrought in the prison. But what about James? The Word says that he was killed. Some of us must die, while others are set free in a miraculous way. But whether I live or die, to God be the glory!

As for me, I went home and continued to put up with a rebellious woman who mocked my God and made a fool of me. I believed that I had to put up with it: partly because of my codependency, partly because I knew the trouble I would be in with the supervisors in my denomination if Blanca did divorce me, and partly because I didn't want two little girls to grow up without their father. The last reason was of the greatest importance to me.

It was noon when Blanca came home for lunch. As calmly as I could, I asked her to tell me the truth about her relationship with my best friend. She looked at me like I was a nut and proceeded to tell me that nothing had happened. Then she asked why I was making all this up. "Who told you such lies?" she demanded. Little did she know that the informant was her own daughter, the child she had always tried to keep away from me.

That night I went to Harrisburg, Pennsylvania, to see my friends, Reverend and Mrs. Emilio Martinez. I knew that I could trust them. Very few people knew the hell that I was living in, but Emilio and Ana were people I would trust with my life.

As I sat in the chair fighting back tears, I tried to explain what had happened, but I simply couldn't. Finally Brother Martinez said, "Angel, you have to let it out. You cannot hold this in. Go ahead, now, and let it out. We are here in my office; no one will hear you."

I got up from my chair and walked around the room. First I punched the wall; then I just broke down. I fell on the floor screaming and crying. Sister Martinez knelt on the floor in front of me and held me in her arms, like a mother holding her crying child.

I could not control myself, and furthermore, I didn't want to. All the years of pain and sorrow came pouring out. Mother, the streets, my home, my wife, my children—it all came out. I stood up and cried unto the Lord. "God, I'm tired of suffering! I'm tired of the pain! When, when will all this end?"

Again I fell to the floor. As I cried out to God, over and over I entreated Him, "Let me live again. Oh, God! Let me live again!"

Reverend Martinez let me pour out my soul. Then he cautioned me, "Don't make any decisions right now, Angel. Try to stay calm." That was easier said than done.

I returned home that night and lay down on the sofa. Everyone was sleeping, so I got a pillow and tried to sleep. The hours seemed like weeks, and the silence of the night made it even worse. I kept thinking that this was just a nightmare, a bad dream—that I would wake up any minute and it would all be over. But this was real, *very* real. My whole world was coming to an end, and I could not stop it no matter how hard I tried.

A few months later I learned that the affair with this friend was not my wife's first affair. Finally Blanca admitted the truth about her affair, but she did not do so to aid the healing of our marriage. Instead she insisted that it was over between us. She told me that she did not like the type of person I had become since I had accepted the Lord. She said that she liked the old Angel. Then Blanca presented this proposition: "Make up your mind. Decide between me and your God. The only way we can get together again is if you resign your God and come back to me." I had to choose between God and Blanca, between the woman I loved with all my heart and the God I loved with all my being.

I looked across the dining room table at my wife and without any hesitation whatsoever spoke these words, *"I will never leave my God, which means that it is over between us. But remember, the day will come when you will regret what you have made me decide today."* With those words I got up, walked out the door, and never returned.

I tried as best as I could to explain to my daughters that Daddy was not going to be living with them any longer. We all cried for a long time. I had put up with so much because I wanted them to have a family, something I never had known. They didn't deserve this pain. They were just two little girls who were full of life and innocence.

Even though our marriage was over, it was another three years before Blanca and I divorced. Our divorce hurt everyone. There were no winners, only losers. This is the way it always is with divorce. It doesn't matter who is at fault; everyone gets hurt, especially the children. God hates divorce and so do I. But sin is like a cancer that eats away at your very soul, causing anyone who yields to it to harden his or her heart against the spouse.

At the time of my divorce, I was an ordained minister with the Assemblies of God denomination. I had started my own speaking and preaching ministry in 1980, and later was recognized by the denomination as a minister. I had kept my superintendent informed of everything that I was going through. He was a man of God, and on different occasions he put his arms around me and prayed for me. One time not long after my marriage with Blanca hit the rocks, he told me that if I divorced and later remarried, I would no longer be able to be a minister with the Assemblies of God. The superintendent and I discussed this at length.

Finally, trying to comprehend this hardship, I responded: "Let me see if I understand this correctly. For many years I have tolerated much from my wife. She has done things to me that only you and I know about. She commits adultery frequently, refuses to repent, and demands a divorce. When I finally decide to pick up my life and remarry, the Assemblies of God will not support me in my decision, but will ask me to resign."

"Yes, Angel," my superintendent responded without hesitation. "You understand our position correctly. The Assemblies of God does not accept remarried ministers, no matter what the circumstances are."

The old saying, "when it rains, it pours," certainly proved to be true in my life. It was only a matter of time until I had to resign and turn in my credentials. Not only did I lose my wife, my kids, and my house, but the organization through which I related to the Body of Christ as a minister of the gospel compounded my misery by giving me my walking papers!

Even though I had been (and still am) an independent evangelist, I was well-known within the Assemblies of God denomination and had preached in just about every church in the district. Rumors began flying around, and I became the topic of conversation for everyone.

When the word got out about my marital problems, many so-called friends simply abandoned me. Crusades were canceled. I was accused of adultery and of abandoning my home. Others said that I had spent too much time on the road and that my wife could not be blamed for divorcing me. Everyone had an opinion as to what had happened, yet because I chose not to expose Blanca, very few knew the full story. Even though there were a few men and women of God within that denomination who secretly encouraged and comforted me, I generally felt entirely alone. People pulled away from me, gave me strange looks as if I had some kind of disease, and treated me more coldly than sinners had done when I was lost. To say that it was a very painful period in my life is an understatement. The only thing that ever hurt me more was the death of my mother.

Many others have suffered what I felt. They too have suffered because of the imperfect world we live in, a world that is full of hate and anger. Many people are still hurting. Oh, how I want Jesus to return!

# Chapter 9

# Mr. Angel Luis Nuñez, Sr.

## (Age 30)

Two weeks after Venus told me about the affair her mother was having with one of my best friends, I had to go to Youngstown, Ohio, to conduct a crusade. I wanted to cancel the event, but they had worked tirelessly in preparation for this crusade and I did not want to disappoint them. Nevertheless, I was destroyed and didn't feel that I even had the strength to stand behind the pulpit, let alone conduct a crusade. Somehow God came through, as He always does, and gave me the strength to preach.

When I arrived for the first service, I locked myself in the pastor's study to pray and did not leave it until it was time to go up to the pulpit to preach. During the day, I kept to myself and assigned my workers to handle everything and leave me alone. Normally I enjoyed socializing with the people, never wanting to be the type of evangelist who was so holy that he couldn't spend even a few minutes with the brothers who had invited him. This time, however, I just didn't have it in me.

On the second day of the crusade, one of my workers came to see me and informed me that there was a lady, Mrs. Alvera, who wanted to talk to me. He said, "I think you had better give this lady some time; she has something very important to tell you."

We set up an appointment, and that afternoon Mrs. Alvera came to see me. She told me that the last time I had been in Youngstown, I had given my testimony, during which I had said that I believed my father had lived in that city some 30 years before. She said that after hearing this information, she had proceeded to look in her telephone book to see if she could find someone by the name of Nuñez. Finding the name of Luis Nuñez, she had called him and had been told that my father had indeed lived in the city some 30 years earlier, but that one day, he simply got up and left. No one had heard from him since.

My visitor also recounted how Luis interrupted her while she was speaking and asked, "How did you get my telephone number?" When Mrs. Alvera then informed him that she had obtained his number from the telephone book, the young man replied, "That's impossible. My phone number is unlisted." When she insisted that she had indeed found the number in the telephone book, he said, "Lady, my number is unlisted; but two years ago the telephone company made a mistake and published my phone number." She then picked up the telephone book and realized that it was two years old. Finally the two agreed to meet. When they met, Mrs. Alvera told Mr. Luis Nuñez my story and informed him that I would be coming to town. She said that she would try to set up a meeting between us. "Maybe, just maybe, we are brothers," Luis agreed.

I was intrigued by her story and temporarily forgot my marital problems. I agreed to meet Luis to see if he and I were related. We set up the meeting, and I went to his apartment. When I knocked on the door, a man about my size answered the door. We looked at each other and told our life stories. I found out that I was one day older than Luis, and that our stories were very similar. We both had a father who had simply walked out on us. He told me that he had some aunts in upstate New York who could verify if we were truly brothers. Since I had a copy of my testimony, which I had recorded on cassette, I gave it to Luis so he could take it to the aunts.

Two weeks later I received a phone call from Luis. "You're not going to believe this, but you are my brother! I took the tape to New York and had my aunts, rather our aunts (we had the same father, but different mothers), listen to it. They confirmed it! *My father is your father. We are* _brothers!_" I let the impact of what Luis said settle in me. Then he said, "You won't believe what our aunts did," he went on, "they flew to Puerto Rico, went to our father's house, sat him down on a chair, and played the tape for him without letting him know who it was from. He listened to your story and started to cry. He wants to see you. His name is Angel Nuñez, Sr."

After I hung up the phone, I started praising the Lord. "You are wonderful," I cried. "I lose one family and You give me another." Then I called my sister. "Maria, Maria!" I said. "Are you sitting down?"

"What is it?" she asked. "Why are you so excited?"

"Maria, you're not going to believe this, but I have just found our father—our real father!" She could hardly contain her joy. We were so excited that we couldn't stop talking.

A few days later we received a letter from Mr. Nuñez in which he expressed his desire to meet us. We made arrangements to go to Puerto Rico to meet him. As far as I was concerned, I no longer hated my father. I guess to a certain extent my sister, in her own way, had also forgiven him.

We packed our suitcases and purchased our tickets, but in our rush to get to Puerto Rico, we forgot the letter that Mr. Nuñez had sent us. The arrangements were that he would pick us up at the airport in Puerto Rico, so we didn't think it was too great an oversight. When we arrived in Puerto Rico, however, I suddenly realized something that we had overlooked. Turning to my sister, I asked, "Maria, how will we know who he is?"

"I don't know. Maybe he will have a sign or something," she surmised.

No one was allowed to meet the plane upstairs in the terminal. As before, everyone had to wait outside the baggage claim area. So after we picked up our bags, we worked our way out to where the people stood waiting. There must have been a few hundred people gathered in that area, and to our dismay, we could not find anyone with a sign. We looked into peoples' faces to see if any of them looked like us, but to no avail. After more than two hours of unrewarded effort, we realized that we had missed our father. So we rented a car and tried to find his house. This too posed a problem, since we had forgotten the letter on which his address was written. All we knew was that he lived in Vietnam, Cataño, Puerto Rico; Vietnam being a neighborhood in Cataño. After driving around for hours, we decided to call it quits for the day and to check into a motel for some much needed rest.

We started looking for a motel and quickly realized there were no motels anywhere in the area. What we did not know was that in Puerto Rico, a motel is a place where you take a prostitute; it is not a place to rest! As I said, we did not know this, so after trying for more than an hour to find a motel, we decided to ask people for directions.

I stopped at a gas station and ask a man about a motel. He looked at my sister in the car, smiled, and then proceeded to give me directions. We looked in vain for this motel but couldn't find it. So I stopped at another gas station and again asked for directions. This man also looked at my sister, smiled, and gave me directions. When we still could not find the motel, I told my sister, "This is crazy; I am going to stop a cop and get some help." About a mile down the road, I found a police officer and told him our frustrations. The officer looked at my sister, smiled, and said, "Sure, buddy, I bet you are desperate to find a motel." Then he gave me directions to an area where three motels were located. I thanked him, shook his hand, and returned to my car. The police officer surprised me as he gustily said, "Enjoy yourself! Have fun!"

"Why is he telling me to have fun?" I asked myself and Maria. She had no clue, but we drove as directed.

I pulled into the driveway of one of the motels and a gentleman came out to see me. He looked at me and my sister, then he said, "I have rooms for $18, $25, and $39." I asked, "Do these rooms have two beds?" He looked at me like I was nuts and asked, "Why do you want two beds? You only need one." I was too tired to argue, so I told him to give me the room for $25. He told me to pull into a garage. When I did, he closed a gate behind me and told me that the entrance to my room was through the garage.

I grabbed the bags and told my sister, "Finally, our room!" When we opened the door to the room, we suddenly realized why everyone had looked at us so funny. The walls of the room were filled with mirrors. Our bed was about four feet high, and romantic music was coming out of the wall. Realizing what kind of a place it was, we started to laugh. As we reflected on everything we had told people and everything they had told us, we laughed even harder. "No wonder they kept looking at you," I told Maria. "And no wonder they told you to enjoy yourself," she replied. We laughed so hard that we barely slept that night.

The next morning we got up and went to the post office to see if they could help us locate our father. The postmaster said that he understood our dilemma but he could not give us any information, since it would violate federal law. But he did offer some good advice. "Go to Vietnam, drive around the area, and try to locate the letter carrier. He should know your father." It was a shot in the dark, but we went for it.

We drove around for half an hour before we finally located the mailman. "Yes, I know Angel Nuñez. As a matter of fact," he said, pointing at me, "you look just like him." He gave us the address and we drove right up to the house.

I stopped the car and looked at my father's house. It was an unusually small two-story house. The first story was made of cement, the second of wood. There was an old, beat-up car in the front. It was obvious that my father was doing poorly. I knocked on the door, but no one answered. "He isn't here," I said to myself. Then I turned around and found myself looking at a little old lady.

"Who are you?" she questioned. "I am Angel Nuñez, Jr." I answered. "Oh, yes, he has been waiting for you. He missed you at the airport and has been trying to find out what happened yesterday. Come over to my house. You can wait for him there."

So Maria got out of the car and we went to this lady's house to wait for our father. The lady introduced herself and offered us some coffee. Her house was a small shack made out of wood, and she was even poorer than our father, but she was warm and friendly. As we talked, chickens walked around our feet in the shack and mosquitoes tried to bite us. And the heat was unbearable! Still I felt good because this was the land of our forefathers, and I thanked God for being there. To me, Puerto Rico was beautiful. I loved to be sitting among my people, drinking coffee, and playing with chickens. _Puerto Rico, la Isla del Encanto!_ (Puerto Rico, the Island of Enchantment!)

Our new friend informed us that our father was not married and that he lived alone. He did have some family who visited him from time to time. We told her a little about ourselves and let her know that we didn't even know how our father looked. We asked her to identify him for us when he returned.

An hour later, our father returned home. As he walked down the street, the little old lady pointed him out to us. I came out of her house and started walking behind him. Then, as he was getting ready to open his gate, I called out his name: "Angel...Angel Nuñez."

He turned around, and to both our amazement, it was like looking into a mirror. He looked like me, just a little older.

*For the first time in my life, I was standing face to face with my father!* He looked at me and knew who I was. We ran to each other and hugged. Maria, coming right behind me, also hugged and kissed him. We also cried for awhile.

I told him honestly, "I have waited a long time for the day that I would meet you. I hated you for a very long time and fantasized about the moment when I would kill you for all the pain you caused my mother. But I want to tell you that Jesus has changed my life. You were not there for me when I needed you, but He was. It was He who watched every step I took. I no longer hate you, Father; love has taken its place and I would like to start a relationship with you 'cause you are my dad." Our father accepted what I said that day and we made our peace. We buried the past and started anew. Then we spent six wonderful days of sharing and of getting to know one another.

Six months later, I returned to Puerto Rico to conduct a crusade in Bayamon. Bayamon is about ten miles from my father's house. We rented a baseball stadium and had five glorious nights of services. Our crusade was transmitted via radio to all Puerto Rico.

The last day of the crusade, I sensed that God was doing something special. The altar was full, and although I had already gave the invitation to those who wanted to accept Jesus, I felt that I should continue making the invitation. Then I saw a man walking toward me. The closer he got, the more I realized who he was: It was my father. He was coming forward to receive Jesus Christ as his personal Savior.

We prayed the sinner's prayer together, then I invited my father to come up on the platform with me. There we placed our arms around each other and cried our hearts out. Since the crusade was live on radio, the switchboards were lit up as people from all over the island called in and accepted the Lord. It was a very special moment, but few people really knew what was happening on the platform where my father and I wept together.

After 35 years, I had finally met my father. Now, after 55 years, my father finally met his Father.

# Chapter 10

# Deborah and I

## *(Age 32)*

Almost three years had passed since my divorce from Blanca and I had to decide what I would do with my life. I still loved her and couldn't forget her, but I had just learned that she had become involved in yet another relationship. So I decided to go into a retreat and ask God to take her from my heart once and for all.

I spent a few days with the Lord, just Him and me. During this time of seclusion, the Lord spoke to me again and reminded me of all His promises. He promised that He would bless me, that He had seen my faithfulness, and that He would heal my heart completely. As I lay on the floor of that room, I felt a powerful hand reach down into my heart and take out all remaining love for Blanca. When I got up, I knew that Blanca was forever removed from my life.

On the way home from my retreat, I decided to stop at Reverend Martinez's church and say hello. When I arrived, I was escorted to his office where, after a few minutes, he came to see me. As I was talking with him, his daughter, Deborah, came into the office to ask her father a question. When she walked across the room, the Holy Spirit spoke to my heart: "Do you see her?" _Yes_, I responded. "I am going to give her to you; she is going to be your wife," God replied. Like Sarah, in her response to the Lord, I burst out laughing in disbelief.

Neither Reverend Martinez nor his daughter understood why I suddenly erupted with laughter, and I didn't explain the outburst. In fact, I didn't tell anyone what had happened to me. I surely wasn't going to say, "The Lord just told me that you are going to become my wife." Deborah would have thought that I was crazy. So I just kept it to myself and prayed about it. This, I am sure, is the best way to handle such matters.

This was not the first time I had met Deborah. About six months earlier, while in Harrisburg, Pennsylvania, taking care of ministerial business, I decided to go to a friend's home and pick up some materials for the next crusade. As I was parking the car, I looked toward the front door of my friend's home, and to my amazement, saw a beautiful woman standing there! She seemed to be waiting for someone.

I parked the car, got out, and started walking up the steps. For a brief moment our eyes met. I said hello and walked on by, but from that moment on, I was entranced by her beauty and kept saying to myself, "This woman is truly beautiful!"

Once inside, I asked my friends about the lady who had been standing at their front door. They told me that she was Reverend Emilio Martinez's oldest daughter, Deborah. She had recently come back from college and was waiting for a ride. Brother Martinez was my best friend and I respected him very much; but he had never told me about his beautiful daughter.

Soon after I stopped by his office on the way home from my retreat, Brother Martinez invited me to come over one evening for dinner. I arrived at the appointed hour and was received at the door by his beautiful daughter. Once again, ours eyes met and I was overwhelmed by her amazing physical beauty. Brother Martinez came to the door just then and said, "Angel, I want to formally introduce you to my oldest daughter, Deborah." I shook her hand and muttered, "Nice meeting you," or something equally lame.

After dinner we were all talking together. It was then that Deborah and I started to develop a friendship. The thought came to my mind that maybe we could take our friendship further...but I brushed it aside. *This girl is too young for me,* I reasoned. After all, most of my friends were five to ten years older than I. Deborah, in contrast, was over seven years younger than I. I had never dated a younger woman in all my life, so thoughts of romance were quickly squelched. *Yes, she is beautiful but too young,* I thought as I departed from the Martinez home that evening. *Besides, she is my best friend's daughter, and I don't know if he would approve of me as a prospective son-in-law!* So I tried to put lovely Deborah out of my mind.

A few months later, I had a big crusade in Vineland, New Jersey. As part of my ministerial board, Sister Ana Martinez, Deborah's mother, was asked to help me with the event. Sister Ana was in charge of coordinating the ushers and the altar workers. For this crusade, Deborah, or Debbie as the family called her, came with her mother to help with the crusade.

During the days that followed, Debbie lent her expertise with a camera and assisted in other areas as needed. I observed her during those few days and was most impressed that she wasn't in awe of my reputation. Many women tend to idolize an evangelist when the anointing is upon him and God uses him in a mighty way. But Debbie seemed to accept me as a regular human being, perhaps because both of her parents are anointed ministers. She was interested in getting to know me better, however.

After the Vineland crusade, Debbie and I became close phone friends. We often spoke for hours as she opened up her heart to me and told me of her dreams and desires. Without her knowing it, what she described as being her dreams and desires were also mine. As I listened to her talk, I would find myself saying, *Wait a minute. Those are my dreams too.* It was as if she had opened my heart while I was asleep and had seen all my innermost desires. Eventually I started to see her as a mature young lady, and her age no longer mattered. But through all of this, I told her neither what the Lord had told me about us nor how I was beginning to feel about her. Besides that, Deborah had a boyfriend. One day she asked for my counsel whether or not she should marry him.

At the time Deborah didn't know my inner thoughts as we spoke of the decision she had to make. All the while I was thinking: *Just my luck! I've found the woman whom I've always wanted and she doesn't even know I like her. Everything she wants in life is what I want, and she has come to me for help! If I encourage her to marry this guy, I will lose her; but if I encourage her to leave him, then later reveal my feelings, she will say that I betrayed her, and I might still lose her!*

I was in a quandary. Finally I decided not to advise her either way, as it could only hurt our relationship. "I can't advise you either way," I said, biting my tongue. "You and the Lord will just have to decide." I did not tell her anything of my feelings. I just gave it to the Lord. If, in time, Debbie chose to leave her boyfriend, then I would tell her how I was feeling.

The wait seemed endless. One night after talking to her for a number of hours, I wrote Debbie a poem that I never intended to give her. It read:

### Pretty Lady,

*I had a dream I could not bear.*
*I closed my eyes and you were there.*
*I tried to hold you in my arms,*
*but all I found were empty palms.*

*I looked again in my despair,*
*to see if you were truly there;*
*and yes, you were just like before,*
*the only thing I could not touch.*

*It was then that I understood*
*that with my eyes I could look,*
*but with my hands I would never hold*
*the pretty lady whom I see*
*every time I have a dream.*

*I long for the day when I awake*
*and you are there*
*...for real, forever.*

*Yours,*
*Angel*

I never sent my poem. I didn't want to go through another painful situation, so I repressed my longings. But the word of the Lord kept ringing in my ears, "I am going to give her to you. She will be your wife."

Debbie made the right decision and God put us together. Our love has been a very special love, and I can say that I have found true happiness. When we told her parents, they simply smiled and told us that they had known this for some time because God had already told them. The funny thing about this is that the woman who held me in her arms as I cried for Blanca became my mother-in-law. God has a sense of humor!

The day was July 2, 1988. On that memorable day, Deborah and I were wed and dedicated our marriage to the Lord. The wedding was beautiful. We had over 350 guests, 2 limos and a Rolls Royce for the bride! I couldn't afford it, but I had always wanted a big wedding. Besides that, I wanted the world to know that it pays to be faithful to God. I wanted everyone to see my victory. I wanted everyone to know it is possible to live again!

God did not fail me. Nor will He fail you. He healed my hurts, just like He will heal yours. For 32 years I lived in pain, but He took away the pain. The true peace I now have is the peace that the Lord had given me at the time of my salvation. But I had longed for someone to love me, flesh of my flesh. The Lord found her for me and we have made a wonderful home together. We are completely fulfilled as husband and wife.

The Lord has also blessed us with three beautiful children: Angela, Israel, and Isaac. He gave me Angela to help me recover those years that I did not have with my girls, Venus and Georgina. He gave me a little boy, Israel, who looks just like me and even wants to be a preacher like me someday! I had always wanted a little boy; with Israel my hope was fulfilled. Then God put the icing on the cake. He gave us Isaac (Hebrew for "laughter"). From the moment he was born, Isaac has lived up to his name. He is always laughing. He is such a warm, caring boy, and so full of joy!

I want the world to know that Jesus never fails! I want you to understand that there are times when God chooses not to tell us why. Why must this happen? Why did I lose my child, my wife? In His wisdom, He chooses not to answer. Ours is not to ask and complain, but rather to trust and obey. Sooner or later He will do His will in your life and you will praise Him.

I had found the woman whom I always longed for. We were made for each other. It is unbelievable! God has placed us together like hand-in-glove. To God be the glory!

I have met countless people in my travels who are hurting, crying, and asking why. I have been able to touch their lives with my life—not because I read it in a book or went to school and studied it, but because I understand from experience the pain and hurt they are suffering. This is why I say, with another follower who suffered greatly for his Master: *"From henceforth let no man trouble me: for I bear in my body the marks of the Lord Jesus"* (Gal. 6:17).

I am so thankful to say that I am alive again. I can now go to the park and the woods and look at nature, seeing the birds and butterflies and enjoying the green grass. I can again stand up and sing to the world a new song, for I am truly alive. When I turn around, this time I see my wife and my children (both young and old) beside me. Then I have no choice but to look up to Heaven and say, "Thank You, Lord, for allowing me to live again."

# Afterword

## *The Crusade Ministry*

When I attended an evangelistic crusade in my mother's church as a five-year-old boy, the guest speaker called me to come forward and anointed me with oil. Then he prophesied, *"This boy will grow up to become a great preacher in the last days."* Things similar to this often happened before Mother died.

When I was seven years old, I would assemble what few dolls my sister owned, along with a couple of my puppets, and would "preach" to them using a "microphone" made from a broomhandle covered with aluminum foil. In these "meetings," Maria would play the tambourine and lead the singing.

As a boy I also dreamt sometimes that I was preaching to thousands of people in arenas, in football stadiums, and in baseball parks. Even while I was running from God, these dreams would sometimes return.

After I was saved in Puerto Rico, doors opened all over the island for me to preach and share the Word of God in all kinds of churches. People who were mature in the Lord would say, "Angel, God has called you to preach. You should take heed to your calling."

I started traveling in the United States with Evangelist Amancio Vizcarrondo. This mighty man of God prayed for people and saw hundreds of people slain in the Spirit and many miracles of all kinds. It was a great training time for me.

After that period, I settled permanently in the U.S. Soon several churches at a time were coming together to hear me preach. Since 1981, I have been in full-time ministry. It has been my privilege to preach all over the U.S., mainly in Spanish-speaking churches, as well as in other countries. I have also had the opportunity of pastoring in Lancaster, Pennsylvania, and in Baltimore, Maryland. Even then, however, I took trips to hold crusades in Mexico, Central America, the Caribbean, and other places.

What has always been exciting for me is how God, time after time, anoints the messages and draws hurting souls to the Cross in an incredible way! We have seen astonishing moves of God in our crusades—people coming to the Lord from all walks of life, giving their broken lives to Him, and receiving peace through the blood of Jesus. My burden is to reach the downcast, the downtrodden, the bruised, and the broken. Jesus is glorified when people come to Calvary!

In a crusade in the South Bronx, a man came to the meeting intent on finding there a man who had wronged him. He purposed to knife his enemy during the service. When he found his target listening attentively to my sermon, he slipped behind him, ready to stab him. At the precise moment that he was readying his knife, I hollered from the platform, knowing only that the Holy Spirit was directing me, "Don't do that! Don't stab him! Forgive him!"

The would-be assailant, shocked out of his wits, dropped his knife, came forward, and followed me in the sinner's prayer. After he gave his life to Jesus, he gave me his knife. I still own that knife.

Another time, during a crusade attended by more than 3,000 people in Houston, Texas, a lady came to the service intent on shooting me. One of my ushers, led by the Holy Spirit, walked down the aisle, went right to her, and grabbed the gun from her just before she would have pulled the trigger.

Another night in a church in New Jersey, the Holy Spirit urged me to command a lady bound to a wheelchair to rise up and walk. No sooner had I said this, then she jumped up, completely healed. She immediately began to run (not walk) with both hands held high in the air.

During another crusade in Texas, the Holy Spirit impressed me to raise my hands and to begin praising the Lord, rather than continuing with the sermon. As I obeyed, people ran to the front, giving their hearts to Jesus and receiving the baptism in the Holy Ghost.

Sometimes there have been intense confrontations with the demonic. During a crusade in Springfield, Massachusetts, three or four people suddenly fell to the ground, wallowing under demonic control. One girl in the front was seized by a spirit and began running out of the service. I knew that the devil was trying to kill her, so I chased her down and grabbed her by the arm at the front door. The demon in her looked at me and said, "I'm going to kill her!" Knowing that the power of the Lord was upon me in a mighty way, I said, "Listen, demon, you let her go right now." Instantly, at that very moment, the demonized girl dropped to the floor. When she got up, she was in her right mind.

In 1986 I was invited to a youth retreat at a campground. For four days and nights the power of God shook us all. God gave me powerful words for those young people, words of knowledge and wisdom (see 1 Cor. 12:8) that impacted their lives in such a way that all 170 young people at the retreat went back to their churches and set the Spanish Eastern District of the Assemblies of God on fire. They went out and won between 4,000 and 5,000 other young people to the Lord, as evidenced in their later gatherings. Eleven years later, the revival that began at that retreat is still going on in many lives!

I want everyone to know that the hem of the Master's garment can dry any tears. If the Lord is for you, no one can stand against you! My testimony does not consist of a man puffing himself up; rather it is one of a man kneeling before the feet of his Master, thanking Him for the great things He has chosen to do in and through His servant, Angel Luis Nuñez.

# Angel L. Nuñez Ministries

is a bilingual ministry bringing unity
to the Body of Christ.

Our vision is to restore with love the broken, hurting, and rejected person into a full and mature relationship with our Lord and Savior, Jesus Christ. The result of this new relationship is to be manifested in the daily living of all who receive Him, as a witness to the world of the power of God in the life of the believer.

To fulfill this vision, we hold conferences, present a singing ministry that includes testimony and draws believers into worship through praise and worship songs, and offer a collection of more than 50 Spanish and English tapes and CDs. This collection includes the following:

## Preaching Tapes
How Shall This Be?
Brokenness
Pure Heart
This Time With Him

## Conference Tapes
New World Order (prophetic)
Who Controls Your Mind? (occult toys)
Are You a Chicken or an Eagle (inner healing)
Sex Before Marriage (for youth)

**Testimony Tape**
Let Me Live Again

**Music CD (English)**
Divine Love

For a complete listing of English and Spanish tapes, or for information concerning any other aspect of our ministry, please call us or write to us at:

**Angel L. Nuñez Ministries**
**P.O. Box 1224**
**Baltimore, MD 21203**
**(410) 675-7256/675-1021 (telephone)**
**(410) 558-2933 (fax)**

# Other
## *Destiny Image titles*
you will enjoy reading

## THE BATTLE FOR THE SEED
*by Dr. Patricia Morgan.*

The dilemma facing young people today is a major concern for all parents. This important book of the 90's shows God's way to change the condition of the young and advance God's purpose for every nation into the next century.

ISBN 1-56043-099-0 $9.99p

## THE FATHERLESS GENERATION
*by Doug Stringer.*

The young people of today have many names—generation X, the lost generation, and the "fatherless generation." With this book Doug Stringer will stir your heart and enflame your desire to reach this generation—and thus the nation—with an invitation to return to *the* Father! *The Fatherless Generation* presents the depth of the need and the hope of the solution—a relationship with Almighty God, our Father.

ISBN 1-56043-139-3 $8.99p

## THE CROSS IS STILL MIGHTIER THAN THE SWITCHBLADE
*by Don Wilkerson.*

Don Wilkerson, co-director of the original Brooklyn Teen Challenge with his brother David, tells of the ministry's incredible growth and success in working with troubled youth today. With current eyewitness reports and testimonies of former addicts and gang members, he proves that *The Cross Is Still Mightier Than the Switchblade*.

ISBN 1-56043-264-0 $9.99p

**Available at your local Christian bookstore.**

**Internet: http://www.reapernet.com**

# Exciting titles
## by Myles Munroe

### IN PURSUIT OF PURPOSE

Best-selling author Myles Munroe reveals here the key to personal fulfillment: purpose. We must pursue purpose because our fulfillment in life depends upon our becoming what we were born to be and do. *In Pursuit of Purpose* will guide you on that path to finding purpose.
ISBN 1-56043-103-2 $9.99p

### UNDERSTANDING YOUR POTENTIAL

This is a motivating, provocative look at the awesome potential trapped within you, waiting to be realized. This book will cause you to be uncomfortable with your present state of accomplishment and dissatisfied with resting on your past success.
ISBN 1-56043-046-X $9.99p

### RELEASING YOUR POTENTIAL

Here is a complete, integrated, principles-centered approach to releasing the awesome potential trapped within you. If you are frustrated by your dreams, ideas, and visions, this book will show you a step-by-step pathway to releasing your potential and igniting the wheels of purpose and productivity.
ISBN 1-56043-072-9 $9.99p

### MAXIMIZING YOUR POTENTIAL

Are you bored with your latest success? Maybe you're frustrated at the prospect of retirement. This book will refire your passion for living! Learn to maximize the God-given potential lying dormant inside you through the practical, integrated, and penetrating concepts shared in this book. Go for the max—die empty!
ISBN 1-56043-105-9 $9.99p

## Available at your local Christian bookstore.

### Internet: http://www.reapernet.com

# O ther
## *Destiny Image titles*
## you will enjoy reading

# **D** *Destiny Image*
# New Releases

# LET ME LIVE AGAIN

## The Morning After the Storm

*Death* is a frightening, isolating word. When cancer took th
mother of eight-year-old Angel Nuñez, his secure, happy child
hood ended. Alone and afraid, Angel faced a new, cruel world o
foster homes, state institutions, and the streets. His innocenc
was shattered. He grew into an angry young man who seethe
with hate and resentment. The last flicker of life within him wa
extinguished by the drugs and violence that surrounded him.

One day, Angel met the Lord Jesus Christ, who gave him a ne
life and a reason to live it. Angel found that the Lord was faithfu
even to see him through the trials of his early ministry and th
loss of his wife and children, because at his moment of deepes
despair, Angel turned to God and cried out, "Take away this pair
and please...let me live again!"

ANGEL L. NUÑEZ is the senior pastor of th
Spanish Christian Church of Baltimore. His wife
Deborah, is the daughter of Bishop Emilio Ma
tinez, and they have three beautiful children–
Angela, Israel, and Isaac. Angel's life is dedicate
to helping people to come to know his wonderfu
life-giving Savior.

## TREASURE HOUSE

An Imprint of Destiny Image
*"For where your treasure is,
There will your heart be also."* Matthew 6:21
P.O. Box 310, Shippensburg, PA 17257-0310

ISBN 1-56043-310-8          Printed in the U.S.A.

See us on the Internet:
http://www.reapernet.com

For Worldwide Distributio